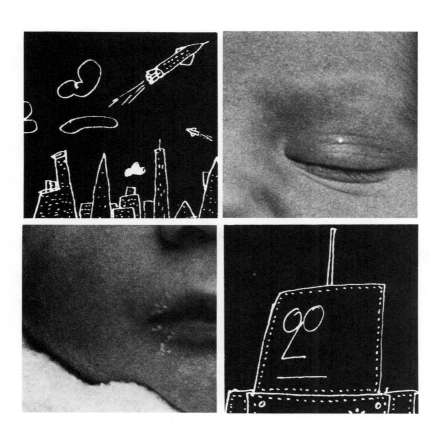

To Edna and Ingeborg
for the support they lent and the
weekends they gave up.
To Suzy
who has a lot of future to grok.
To Dad
who represents the best of the past.
To Allan Maclear,
"Mac," friend, counselor, and editor
ex officio.

GROKKING THE FUTURE
SCIENCE FICTION IN THE CLASSROOM
BERNARD C. HOLLISTER
DEANE C. THOMPSON
PFLAUM/STANDARD

ACKNOWLEDGMENTS

Many thanks to Allan Maclear, who suffered through the reading of the manuscript and offered numerous constructive criticisms. Thanks to Edna Hollister for typing much of the manuscript, and thanks also to Bill Campbell for the help he gave on the Willowbrook Survey.

Illustrations by Arthur Asa Berger
Photography by Wallowitch
Book Design by Joe Loverti

TABLE OF CONTENTS

INTRODUCTION

This book has two objectives. One is to demonstrate how science fiction (Sf) offers new insights into current social issues, and the other is to help students become more creative in their thinking about the future, thus increasing their options for tomorrow. Ideally, we would like to help our students, in Robert Heinlein's term*, to "grok" the future — to grasp it with all their senses and all their being. We can't take them via time machine to tomorrow, but we can offer alternatives, through Sf, for grokking the future.

Why does a country as well informed and as self-conscious as the United States allow its social problems to reach the flash point before action is taken? Certainly this happened with the environmental issue. We see this kind of "crisis management" with urban decay, the proliferation of the automobile, and the disappearance of suburban open space, to name only a few current examples. One reason has to be that for many decades we embraced the idea that rapid industrial and technological progress is the prime value, with hardly a nod toward the social consequences. Public apathy is another factor, and this is compounded by the increasing bigness of our institutions. In the shadow of big government, the giant university, or the gargantuan corporation, many of us feel we don't really count; we are simply inconsequential numbers — ciphers — in a constellation of anonymous millions. This belief may be reinforced by our frustrating attempts to resolve picayune matters, such as getting a company to correct a computerized bill, or attempting to penetrate the labyrinth of bureaucratic buck-passing to have the corner street light fixed.

The situation is further complicated by media which bombard us into electronic numbness with programs about "social problems," transforming us into near-zombies who observe the passing scene with jaded senses and then, with a resigned shrug of the shoulders, lapse back into apathy.

For years protesting youth have been prominently displayed on the evening TV news, leading us to conclude perhaps that the young are more socially aware than their elders. But are they? One of the most important needs in education, and particularly in the social studies, is hard data about student attitudes toward social problems. Since

---

*In Stranger in a Strange Land

we often lack such data, we are forced into the elusive world of supposition, conjecture, and stereotypic generalizations about young people.

To get some clearer reading of student views and concerns at Willowbrook High School, we decided to give a survey (Appendix 2) to collect some demographic data on the number of children in our students' families, how many cars their families owned, etc. At the same time, we were seeking attitudinal information on such topics as students' optimism or pessimism about the nation's future, and their attitudes toward pollution, over-population, and other social problems. We hope that other teachers in inner city schools, rural communities, and other areas would administer this survey also, or a similar one, and we would then have material for comparison.

The survey helped us realize which social problems the students were already aware of — for example, environmental deterioration — and consequently we can spend time concentrating on ways of improving these conditions. On the other hand, students are not so attuned to the increasing mechanization of American society, and we feel we have a responsibility to bring this situation to the students' attention. Of course, there is a danger that students will become more pessimistic as they confront additional problems, but our belief is that recognition of the real dimensions of a problem necessarily precedes its resolution. Also, we don't teach every one of the units in this book to every student, thus avoiding "crisis overload."

Grokking the Future

Grokking the Future offers ways to approach social issues through Sf. Through the creative eyes of the good science fiction writer, social problems can be viewed with fresh insights and the problems become challenges. Unfortunately, many people stopped paying attention to Sf back when bug-eyed monsters cavorted after scantily clad girls, or when Buck Rogers and Flash Gordon zapped their adversaries with ray guns. Though many students enjoy Sf as a genre, they sometimes fail to realize that serious commentaries are being made in Sf about both the present and the future. The Sf writer certainly allows us to see the future through a glass darkly, but he often allows us to see it through a glass clearly, too. It is only in retrospect that we claim the genius of insight for the Sf writer whose predictions were accurate, but let us not discount the absurd predictions, particularly when they jar us into new insights about the future.

Happy grokking!!!!!

Bibliographic Note

The sources for the short stories and novels cited are at the conclusion of each chapter. Since almost all of the sources are currently published paperbacks, the publisher is given but not the price or date of production. It has been our experience that paperback prices fluctuate quickly and it becomes useless to give such data. We also feel that, with the current paperbacks, publication dates are not necessary, nor is it always possible to determine from data in the paperback edition the original publication date of a work.

Chapter 1

HOW TO BEGIN

In the Willowbrook Survey, only four percent of the students felt that they had considerable control over the future. These results didn't really surprise us because we were operating with the hypothesis that most young people have not seriously considered the question. Like their elders, they seem to accept the view that the future just happens. Therefore, we think that in any future-oriented units, it is essential that students first speculate on their own relationship with tomorrow. Will they have any control over the future, or will they passively accept whatever comes?

Robert Theobald in Futures Conditional includes three excellent stories which offer different views of man's control over the future: Ray Bradbury's "Sound of Thunder," Isaac Asimov's "What If?" and Robert Heinlein's "Lifeline."

Bradbury's "Sound of Thunder" offers bored hunters of the future "time safaris" to the past where they gun down prehistoric monsters. Paths are laid down through the primordial jungle; the hunters are warned not to stray from these paths for fear that they might disrupt the ecological balance of the past and thus change the future. One erstwhile hunter does stray from the path, steps on a butterfly, and consequently changes not only the evolutionary pattern of the eco-system, but also the future political development of the world. The author's position is that man, if only accidentally, has great power to shape the future.

In Asimov's "What If?" a young couple speculates on what would have happened if they had not met. How many of us ponder this question? The lucky (or are they so lucky?) couple meets a little old man who has a device which allows them to view the past. The couple discovers that they still would have ended up with each other. Asimov's position on the future is that if one chance event had not occurred, other forces would have intervened so that the result would be the same.

If you want to move the discussion of "what if" from the personal realm to greater questions, how about: What if the United States had lost World War II? Parenthetically, there is an Sf novel The Man in the High Castle by Philip K. Dick which deals at length with this theme. What if atomic bombs had never been invented? What if John Kennedy had lived? Still other "What If...?" questions are: What if brain transplants are perfected? What if an individual were allowed to terminate his life at will? What if scientists were able to grow embryos outside of the womb? What if every family were limited to only one automobile? For further "What If...?" suggestions, see Appendix 1.

A final story for this section is Robert Heinlein's "Lifeline," in which the protagonist is able to predict with chilling accuracy the day and date of any person's death. Heinlein's view of the future is conveyed in the words of the popular song "Que Sera, Sera" — "Whatever will be, will be." In this story, unlike Asimov's, man has greater leeway to interact with the impersonal future to change it. A major question for "Lifeline" is, would you want to know your death date?

After reading this story, we often ask students what 10 things they would do if they learned that they would die exactly one year from the present, and we have had some highly personal and deep discussions as a result. In fact, this story and that question nearly always bring the look that we seek so often in education and find so little: "I've never thought about that before."

As suggested in the Introduction, one of our major concerns is to motivate our students to confront the future creatively. We feel that this can best be done by encouraging them to think divergently; to explore as many alternative futures as possible. Convergent thinking already has locked us into set ways and caused us many difficulties. For example, Americans almost always think that the only way to solve the nation's ills is by spending more money. We try to stimulate our students to think of other ways to change the status quo. Unlike so many of us, the Sf writer is not afraid of the bizarre and the unusual and employs it with great relish, and this helps to goad students to think more freely. Therefore, a second introductory unit we offer our students is a mini-unit on creativity.

One way to begin a creativity unit is to give students an idea of the good Sf writer's breadth of vision through the use of a novel like Brian Aldiss' The Long Afternoon of Earth. Aldiss portrays a planet which has stopped rotating so that portions of it are in eternal afternoon, some parts in twilight, and still others in permanent darkness. Vegetative life has come to rule all, eliminating insects, animals, and even the deposed king, man, in the continuous afternoon of earth. To survive, plants have evolved into exotic species: the tummyelms, which look like dead logs but capture and consume plants and animals alike; fungi which take over men's minds; killerwillows which viciously attack anything that moves. Still other plants begin to mock the actions of birds and animals.

Other Sf novels possibly of use in a creativity unit are Frank Herbert's <u>Dune</u>, Ray Bradbury's <u>The Martian Chronicles</u>, or perhaps Tolkien's <u>Lord of the Rings</u>.

We offer the following creativity exercises to complement the readings. Remember, the idea is to make the students more divergent and less convergent in their thinking.

Student Response:

Have students bring in a common household object such as a screwdriver or can opener and describe it to the class as an archaeologist of the future might, the only limitation being that they cannot describe what it actually is in our society. What did these people (of the past) do with this odd object? Does it have aesthetic qualities? Etc.

Have students design and describe inventions of the future.

Have students redesign the human body to reflect the environmental and technological changes they think will happen in the next two hundred years.

Try some of the "What If...?" exercises in Appendix 1.

Design clothes of the future that will reflect what significant changes you see happening in the next two hundred years.

Design the automobile of the future. Or will there even be automobiles?

Find an unfamiliar object or foodstuff and have students deduce all they can about the society which produced the object. For example, if you can find plantain, stalk sugar cane, raw cacao beans, or dried seaweed, bring them in for analysis. What might future foods be like? What changes would occur if we began taking food pills rather than eating actual food?

For objects, you might want to bring in a Japanese tea whisk, art objects, coins, stamps. Have a student describe an object nonverbally.

Have students develop the following sentences into brief Sf short stories:

1. It was the year 2053. Government biologists were desperately fighting to save the last tree east of the Mississippi...

2. On the fourth day of Leisure Month, work riots broke out again...

3. On Labor Day, President Rover addressed the nation about the human problem...
4. The third clone came out perfectly but Chief Biologist Kramer was definitely worried...
5. "If there is anything I can't stand it is a talkative salamander, especially before I've had my morning coffee...
6. He was thirty-five and over-age, but Jack Smith had a false I.D. as he walked up to the Drug Bar...
7. Zandu was really down in the dumps because this was the third cold in his horn this winter...
8. Somehow, although nobody really knows why, a slight crack began to trace its way across the city's life dome last month and...
9. Washington — July 12, 2041...It was reported yesterday by usually reliable government sources that a man was murdered in Chicago...
10. Riots broke out yesterday in San Francisco when it was announced that the first human-robot marriage took place...
11. Duplication Processes, Inc. announced yesterday that their androids built to represent any human, living or dead, were now being priced at only $500.00, with no money down...
12. Los Angeles — 2011...It was reported last night by a local resident that he heard a car...

Students can think up their own introductions and develop them into short stories. Sf short stories don't have to be long; some of the best are just a typewritten page or two in length (300-700 words).

Bibliography

Asimov, Isaac, "What If?", Futures Conditional, Robert Theobald (ed.), Bobbs-Merrill.
Aldiss, Brian, Long Afternoon of Earth, Signet.
Bradbury, Ray, The Martian Chronicles, Bantam.
Bradbury, Ray, "Sound of Thunder," R is for Rocket, Ray Bradbury, Bantam; also in Eco-Fiction, John Stadler (ed.), Washington Square Press.
Dick, Philip, The Man in The High Castle, Popular Library.
Heinlein, Robert, "Lifeline," Futures Conditional, Robert Theobald (ed.), Bobbs-Merrill.
Herbert, Frank, Dune, Ace.
Tolkien, J. R., Lord of The Rings, Ace.

Chapter 2

YOU CAN'T FOOL MOTHER NATURE: ECOLOGY
Environmental Concern—Pressing Need or Passing Fancy?

Americans are much given to fads — in the 1920's it was mah-jongg and flagpole sitting; more recently it has been the hula hoop and Volkswagen stuffing. In much the same way, certain causes are "in" or passé, according to the capricious shifting of public attention. For some time now, it has been "in" to be concerned about ecology, and those with active social consciences have espoused one environmental cause after another. Now, however, before any of our major ecological problems really have been solved, enthusiasm for the cause may be fading. Unfortunately, here in America, if one of our crusades does not immediately capture Jerusalem, we are quick to abandon the effort. We are willing to undertake large tasks, but we want instant results, and undoubtedly it will take decades to soothe our raped environment.

It may be wishful thinking to hope that young people can be sensitized to environmental issues by anything that teachers can initiate at school. Most students will pay lip service to ecological causes — mainly because this is easy to do and costs nothing. In the Willowbrook Survey, for example, 80 percent of the students said they were either "very concerned" or "considerably concerned" about environmental pollution, and 76 percent thought that stiff fines and/or jail sentences should be imposed on polluters. At the same time, only 55 percent favored requiring that food and drink be sold only in returnable containers, and 73 percent said that they were unwilling to limit the ownership of automobiles, the greatest polluters of all. Obviously, many students either don't see that they are part of the problem, or they don't want to be inconvenienced by making any commitment which might involve action.

Action, obviously, is vital, but some environmental education programs designed to stimulate ecological activism among young people appear increasingly ineffective. These programs began to spring up five or six years ago in response to public pressure generated by the media, and now they have proliferated to the point where students can hardly escape them. Naturally, when they are bombarded by so many ecology units, students begin to get bored; as a result, they have become exceedingly difficult to jar out of their acceptance of things as they are.

In short, if the teacher really wants to change student behavior through an ecology unit, something new and fresh will have to be offered. Students need to be shocked and shaken repeatedly; their feet must be held to the fire until they cry out in protest. We use a number of Sf stories to revitalize tired ecology units, and most of them hit students hard.

Explaining the Concept of Ecological Balance

Before explaining how specific environmental issues may be approached through a combination of science fiction and fact, we believe that the basic principle of an eco-system in balance needs to be explained to students. One way to do this is to use all or part of George Stewart's novel, Earth Abides. We have found that, after being introduced to this book, many students will read it on their own because not only is it well suited for instructional purposes, but it's a good story as well. Stewart describes an Earth upon which most of the people have died in a mysterious epidemic, and both the survivors and the planet itself must adjust to the new conditions. Gradually, man's works decay and the remaining inhabitants form themselves into tribes and become part of a balanced eco-system.

Student Response:

Why do the men finally form hunting tribes instead of restoring technological civilization or turning to agriculture? How does equilibrium finally return to the system? Answering these questions increases the student's ability to understand the necessity of ecological balance.

Though Earth Abides certainly can help students to understand the concept of a balanced eco-system, it cannot do the job alone. To further aid students to grasp this idea, the teacher might use one of the many fine films which explain the ecology of a given area (Disney's Nature's Half Acre, for example), or even try his own hand at creating a completely imaginary environment in ecological balance, then

16

asking students to explain the probable effects of certain introduced changes. As a further exercise, students can be assigned to conceive a viable human culture which would fit into this imaginary eco-system.

Frank Herbert's monumental novel, Dune, would be of great help to a teacher in developing an imaginary culture and eco-system. Perhaps this award-winning book is over-long and a little hard to get into because the world it depicts is so alien to us, but the novel is invaluable because it works out an eco-system in full detail. Even better, Herbert brilliantly develops the culture of those who live on the planet Arrakis. The determining factor in shaping both the culture and the ecology of Arrakis is that the planet has almost no water. Beginning with this premise, everything follows naturally. To enter the vast desert regions and survive, even the casual visitor must be equipped with a "stillsuit" which recycles the body's water so well that less than a thimbleful a day is lost. Spitting is a gesture of respect because it sacrifices water; when people die, their body's entire store of water is reclaimed for the tribe.

Student Response:

What kind of animals might live on such a planet? What might be the immediate and long-range effects of introducing large supplies of water? What would common Earth rituals such as tooth brushing or offering a toast at a formal dinner be like if transferred to Arrakis? Stimulate student discussions with questions like these — and see where the students' imaginations lead you.

Herbert includes an appendix in which he explains the ecology of Arrakis, and something of the culture of the Fremen desert dwellers which has been molded by that ecology. It would be a shame to bypass the story itself, but a real insight into the operation of an eco-system can be gained simply by reading the appendix.

Additional Examples of Balanced Eco-Systems

While Dune and Earth Abides are probably the two works which students will find most attractive, other books also will serve to illustrate the basic idea of ecological balance. Brian Aldiss' The Long Afternoon of Earth, described in Chapter 1, is one example. How, students might be asked, have the physical and cultural changes that men have undergone in this story been determined by the environment? Why, for example, are the people now green? Why do they live in small tribes? Why are the tribes so youth-oriented? If men are to continue to survive, what further changes will they have to undergo? Why are there so few animals? Why have those that do remain not died out like the rest? What present-day American customs would have to change in this world?

So far we have suggested only novels which would assist in clarifying for students the concept of a balanced eco-system, but many short stories also would be of help. One of the best of these is "Balanced Ecology," by James Schmitz. Whenever humans land on a new planet they will, of course, introduce a new element into the eco-system, and the system will react. In "Balanced Ecology," the system adjusts by incorporating the first group of humans and reaching a new balance. The system cannot, however, absorb an unlimited number of men safely, and so the system's defense mechanisms proceed to destroy any new arrivals who threaten the newly-achieved equilibrium.

Student Response:

Every detail of this eco-system is worked out, which makes it easy for students to analyze the system and its workings. How are things that die disposed of? How are the various parts of the system interdependent? Where do the humans fit? If you went to the planet, how could you get the balanced eco-system to accept you instead of killing you?

Another story which explains ecological principles by looking at men trying to plant a colony on an alien planet is "Student Body," by F. E. Wallace. The prospective colonists from Earth encounter a creature which they call the "omnimal." This creature is subject to a unique system of evolution which causes important physical changes in the omnimal in months instead of centuries. At first the omnimal is seen as a small, harmless rodent-like creature, but it develops a taste for the settlers' crops. To combat the menace to the food supply, the settlers create robot cats, but the omnimal immediately evolves into a form large enough to defeat the cats. The Earthmen counter with great Dane-sized terriers, only to have the omnimal develop into a tiger. Finally, when the tigers prove to be easy to shoot, the super evolution process creates the most dangerous animal of all — man.

In Wallace's story the colonists decide that they must negotiate with this last creature, but students might be asked to assume that the Earthmen try to kill the latest form of the omnimal as they did the earlier ones. Beginning with this premise, let students write a different ending to the story. Another writing assignment might be to tell students that the omnimal has found its way to Earth by stowing away on a space ship, and that they are to write a story of their own with this as the starting point.

Understanding Symbiosis

Should the teacher wish to illustrate some specific aspect of ecology such as evolution, works like The Long Afternoon of Earth and "Student Body" are ideal. A perfect example of symbiosis, which is vital in the balanced operation of an eco-system, can be found in "Grandpa," also by James Schmitz. "Grandpa" is the nickname given to a kind of living raft which Earthmen settling on another planet use for water transportation. Unknown to them, at one stage of its life cycle Grandpa falls under the direction of another creature whose intentions toward humans are strictly culinary, and by the time the symbiotic relationship is discovered, it is almost too late to prevent Grandpa from having some colonists for lunch.

Student Response:

What examples of symbiosis on Earth can the students find? What happens to one creature when the other is exterminated? Where would the pilot fish be, for example, without the shark, or the rhino with no tick bird to keep him parasite-free?

Human Interference With the Eco-System

After the student has learned something about the functioning of an eco-system, one obvious next step is to ask what occurs when something interferes with it. Case studies of this interference can be found in books like Silent Spring, by Rachel Carson; the popular news magazines have followed the depredation of the crown of thorns starfish on the Great Barrier Reef. In many cases, of course, man has been the destroyer, upsetting the balance and wreaking havoc through ignorance or carelessness. This is a popular theme among Sf writers.

Ray Bradbury, for example, employs it with expertise in "Sound of Thunder" (Chapter 1). This truly fine story has great appeal for students. The last time we used it, we discovered — to our delight — that some of our slowest students not only were enjoying it and getting the point, but were lending copies to their friends to read during lunch hour! Of course, it is a long step from a crushed butterfly to the changed English language and election of a dictator in the U.S. that the story presents. Might these events logically result from the first action? We don't know if Bradbury had an actual chain of resulting changes in mind, but we suggest that students be encouraged to work one out for themselves.

A variation on the theme of human interference with the balance of nature may be found in "Uncalculated Risk," by Christopher Anvil, in which a soil-texturizing agent which seems to be the answer to the world's food shortage instead threatens to turn the entire planet into a mudhole. Another example, although somewhat bizarre, is "To Fell A Tree," by Robert F. Young. This eerie tale is set on a distant planet, the outstanding feature of which is the presence of giant trees as tall as the Empire State Building. Men being men, they fell the trees — only to find that the trees had been

supporting the human colony in a way no one had realized:
by growing the very houses in which the people were living!

Student Response:

At this point students should be asked to find and
report on examples of cases in which well-intentioned human
interference with nature has had undesirable, or even disastrous, results. Such examples are, of course, legion. They
range from the harmful proliferation of imported species of
animals, such as mongooses in Hawaii or rabbits in Australia, to the growing ineffectiveness of the bird-killing pesticides to which crop-damaging insects have become increasingly immune. Scientists are working today to check the
northward advance from Brazil of a strain of viciously ag-
gressive African bees which had been imported for their
honey-making capabilities, but which have escaped from
their hives and killed many people. Learning about similar
incidents will force the students to recognize that we are
dealing with the real world here, not just reading wild stories.

Microbes Also React to Man's Interference

Insects, of course, are not the only creatures which
are able to strengthen themselves against human attacks
through mutations and natural selection. Microorganisms
also do this constantly (each new strain of the so-called
"Asian Flu" is an example); and when we encourage the
process, accidentally or on purpose, there is always the
chance that a new species of microbe might get out of control.
Why else were the early teams of moon-visiting astronauts
quarantined when they returned to Earth? This practice has
been abandoned because the moon seems to have no harmful
visitors to send us, but this does not mean that a laboratory
experiment could not misfire, or that future space travelers
might not inadvertently bring unwanted guests home with them.
This is just what happens in Michael Crichton's best-seller,
The Andromeda Strain.
Plagues have, of course, been known in the past, and
if something like the Andromeda Strain should be loosed upon
the land, it might be no more than we deserve. Perhaps this
is the only way we can ever atone for our savage treatment

of once-beneficent nature. Admittedly, some of the damage we have done has been accidental, as our technology ranges far ahead of our sociology; but much also has been deliberate and uncaring, a result of our almost psychotic drive to dominate.

Nowhere is this destructive spirit better illustrated than in Kurt Vonnegut's "A Deer in the Works." Vonnegut bitterly attacks the American corporation in this story about a young editor who considers closing down his struggling newspaper to work for a giant corporation as a publicity man. His first assignment is to watch the hunt for a deer which somehow managed to get into the plant grounds and, as soon as the terrified animal is slaughtered, to write a story which will bring the company favorable publicity. The reader may rejoice momentarily when the hero lets the deer go and then quits his job, but the total effect of this story is extremely depressing. There is simply <u>no</u> way that the company can get along with nature — no thought that perhaps the deer could be freed.

Although most Americans seldom make a real effort to get along with nature, as Vonnegut's story illustrates, it certainly should be possible for men to live as part of Earth's eco-system without trying to master it. The teacher might call the students' attention to the American Indian, or the Tasaday of the Philippines, as examples of non-technological man in harmony with nature.

Might an Abused Nature Strike Back?

Even <u>with</u> modern technology to help us conquer nature, there are times when the ravaged land goes out of control and strikes back. Many excellent stories can be used to illustrate this situation, including Doris Lessing's "A Mild Attack of Locusts." This story describes the descent, onto a South African farm, of an immense flock of locusts which humans can do little to check.

Then go one step further: if locusts can harm man, why not other creatures as well? Daphne Du Maurier's famous story, "The Birds," is probably known to some students through the Hitchcock film, but it is even more chilling when read. It can be used to suggest that perhaps we ought to stop taking nature's benevolence for granted!

While an attack by billions of birds hardly seems likely (especially if we continue our indiscriminate use of pesticides), and technology might be able to stop a locust plague, so far no one has been able to figure out a way to stabilize the earth's crust. (Of course, this did not stop the U.S. from detonating a huge underground nuclear explosion on Amchitka Island, in the middle of a known earthquake zone!) In Allan Danzig's "The Great Nebraska Sea," a huge geological fault shifts — flooding eight states, creating a great inland sea, and making Denver a port city. Danzig describes a disaster of epic proportions, and also touches on some of the changes that would take place in the American economy as time passed and things began to settle down. Students might be asked to come up with other examples of changes, social as well as economic, which would follow the establishment of so great an internal sea.

Frequently accompanying earth tremors are tidal waves; in some parts of the world, they are an ever-present menace. In "A Stay at the Ocean," Robert Wilson describes a monster tsumani which causes the water level along the coast of the eastern United States to recede for miles. Thousands of sightseers are lured so far out onto the ocean floor that the wave catches them when the tide returns.

Perhaps this view of abused nature finally striking back is a fanciful one — perhaps, too, men have grown too strong and will win the battle! There is little in our history to lead us to think that we are going to reverse ourselves and become effective conservationists; it is far more likely that we will continue on our fatal course until no one can draw an unmasked breath, a clear stream is nothing but a memory, and most species of animals and birds have gone the way of the passenger pigeon.

This is the kind of world depicted in Out There, by Adrien Stautenburg: a world in which most of the people live in great domed cities and dare not venture out without masks and protective clothing. Strangely, this is a semi-hopeful story, as a small party of children, led by an adult who remembers things as they used to be, ventures out on a camping trip into the mountains and finds that nature has begun to make a comeback.

Student Response:

How, students might be asked, would you like to live in such a world? What are you, personally, willing to do — right now — to help reverse the trends which inevitably will bring this future world into being?

Making a Commitment — and Sticking to It

This is one time when students should be pushed to make a personal commitment or take some direct action. They should not be allowed simply to say, "Yes, this would be an awful world and I wouldn't like it" — and then continue to litter and to tolerate three or four automobiles in their families.

Let us warn you in advance that you may experience some frustration here — often it is next to impossible to crack the shell of youthful indifference. Students will give you the "right" answer to assure themselves of a good grade, but often they are reluctant to admit that something studied in school just might have some relevance to the "real" world. Learning comes with doing, and the teacher who only preaches won't get far. Students must be given grades for action they take, not for principles they profess.

This means that the 80 I.Q. student, who cares enough to switch his gasoline purchases to the non-leaded variety and get his engine tuned up to meet government specifications, must get an A for this part of the unit; while the honor student, who can sail through examinations with ease but who will take no real action, must get the F. You will receive plenty of criticism on this grading system. If you really want to change any attitudes, though, this policy is one way to go about it — provided that both teacher and school accept the admittedly controversial view herein implied, that the school should function as an agent for change.

Live Animals — or Electric Pets?

There are many Sf stories dealing with questions of air and water pollution, but few like Out There, which gives equal time to the animal kingdom. Another book on this topic is Do Androids Dream of Electric Sheep? by Philip K. Dick. Dick's hero is a bounty hunter for escaped androids, so this book also deserves mention in Chapter 10. On post-World War III Earth, many people have emigrated to Mars to escape the radiation which has destroyed nearly all animals. Naturally, that which is scarce immediately becomes a status symbol, so not only do today's most common domestic animals bring premium prices, but there is a thriving industry which builds and maintains electric animals which can be told from the real thing only upon close examination. As you can see, this multi-faceted story also could be used in an economics course. There, you'd ask the students such questions as: Name some of today's "status symbols." Are there any "phony" ones? How far do we carry conspicuous consumption today? Do students admit to feeling the need to own something merely because someone else does?

One of the most touching scenes in Dick's story occurs when his hero finds what he believes to be a live toad in the woods, and is overwhelmed with awe. Still more revealing is his intense need to own a real live animal, and when the goat which he risks his life to earn is deliberately killed by a renegade android, we share the hero's pain and shock.

Out There and Do Androids Dream of Electric Sheep? can be used to raise some basic questions about the relationship between men and the so-called "lesser" animals. Will it matter to anyone when the cheetah and the bald eagle are gone forever? Do we have the right to destroy a species for the sake of convenience or amusement? Why do students keep and love pets? Is there some emotional need in people which would go unsatisfied if animals are erased from the earth? Or might we simply substitute electric creations, as in Dick's story? Is this a ridiculous question? Ask your students: What about Disneyland?

Two Views of "The End"

If we continue to show so little regard for our environment, how will it all end? What will be the shape of Armageddon when it arrives? Neatly bridging the gap between fiction and fact, Dr. Paul Erlich provides one answer to this question in "Eco-Castrophe," which is not so much a story as a skillful detailing of disasters which already have taken place and those which easily may happen tomorrow. While it is a bit slow-going in places, "Eco-Castrophe" is not long, and Dr. Erlich's description of a many-sided ecological

Ragnarok is so realistic and plausible that we almost can guarantee that more thoughtful students will get a good healthy scare.

James Blish's picture of the end, in "We All Die Naked," is as detailed and scientifically sound as Dr. Erlich's — and might be more attractive to students because it has a real story line. Carbon dioxide buildup has melted the icecap at the North Pole and raised the level of the oceans so high that New York commuters go to work by boat. One of the most powerful men in this world choked with trash is the head of the garbage workers' union, so he is allowed to choose 10 people to join a select emigration party to carry life to the moon and, eventually, Mars. When he learns that both the earth and moon are headed for the same fate, he and his party choose the manner of their passing: they stand quietly atop a building, watching the first of the earthquakes rock New York.

Student Response:

One of the best uses for "We All Die Naked" is in values education. Ask students: If you could choose 10 people to be saved from a disaster, who would you choose? Why? In Blish's story, did the people who chose to die overlook any alternatives? Would you have made the choice they did, or a different one? Why? Obviously, no student can answer questions like these without learning a good deal about himself.

The Last Man on Earth

To end this chapter on a fitting note, we would like to suggest "Wednesday, November 15, 1967," by George Alex Effinger. Poignant and bitter, this story records the random thoughts of the last man on Earth, as he wrote them on the back of an old calendar before dying and willing the heritage of mankind to any creature able to accept it. This is a profoundly pessimistic story, useful for sheer shock value, for Effinger is merciless and refuses to let the reader off the hook. How would you like to see your wife die from asphyxiation on the subway? Your newborn son die in an hour, because there are no more oxygen masks? Or, as the dying man puts it in his last words,

Summer of my life:
how will I feel when I see
leaves wither and fall?

Yes. Well, I know, I guess.

Bibliography

Aldiss, Brian, The Long Afternoon of Earth, Signet.

Anvil, Christopher, "Uncalculated Risk," Nightmare Age,
    Frederik Pohl (ed.), Ballantine.

Blish, James, "We All Die Naked," Three for Tomorrow,
    Dell.

Bradbury, Ray, "A Sound of Thunder," Eco-Fiction, John
    Stadler (ed.), Washington Square Press; also in R Is for
    Rocket, Ray Bradbury, Bantam.

Crichton, Michael, The Andromeda Strain, Dell.

Danzig, Allan, "The Great Nebraska Sea," Spectrum #4,
    Kingsley Amis and Robert Conquest (eds.), Berkley.

Dick, Philip, Do Androids Dream of Electric Sheep?, Signet.

Du Maurier, Daphne, "The Birds," Eco-Fiction, John Stadler
    (ed.), Washington Square Press.

Effinger, George Alex, "Wednesday, November 15, 1967,"
    The Ruins of Earth, Thomas Disch (ed.), Berkley.

Erlich, Paul, "Eco-Castrophe," Nightmare Age, Frederik
    Pohl (ed.), Ballantine.

Herbert, Frank, Dune, Ace.

Lessing, Doris, "A Mild Attack of Locusts," Voyages:
    Scenarios for a Ship Called Earth, Rob Sauer (ed.),
    Ballantine.

Schmitz, James, "Balanced Ecology," Nebula Award Stories
    1965, Damon Kinght (ed.), Pocket Books; also in Analog 5,
    John Campbell (ed.), Doubleday.

    , "Grandpa," Spectrum #5, Kingsley Amis and
    Robert Conquest (eds.), Berkley.

Stautenburg, Adrien, Out There, Dell.

Stewart, George, Earth Abides, Fawcett Crest.

Vonnegut, Kurt, "A Deer in the Works," The Ruins of Earth,
    Thomas Disch (ed.), Berkley.

Wallace, F. E., "Student Body," Voyages: Scenarios for a
    Ship Called Earth, Rob Sauer (ed.), Ballantine.

Wilson, Robley, "A Stay at the Ocean," Eco-Fiction, John
    Stadler (ed.), Washington Square Press.

Young, Robert F., "To Fell a Tree," A Decade of Fantasy
    and Science Fiction, Robert P. Mills (ed.), Doubleday.

Chapter 3

TO BE OR NOT TO BE: POPULATION
Overpopulation — Here and Now

Isaac Asimov, asked what the earth's future would be like, once gave a one-word answer: "Crowded."

Because overpopulation is the basic cause of most of the ecological and environmental problems described in the previous chapter, the subject deserves special treatment. We have made no attempt to develop a complete population unit which would, of course, contain factual materials as well as the recommended stories. We will mention some non-fiction materials, but this chapter will be confined basically to a discussion of selected Sf works which can be used to pose the problem of overpopulation, explore its facets, or point to some possible solutions. Most of the projected solutions are highly undesirable from one standpoint or another — Sf writers are fond of saying, in effect: "If population growth is not checked soon by relatively acceptable means, this shocking method will ultimately have to be adopted...take steps now, or this could happen." Let us pay heed.

It is advisable to start students who may be new to science fiction with a view of the future which is not too alien to the world of today. A study of overpopulation problems might best begin with stories which avoid settings on other planets or projections into far-distant centuries. "Billenium," by J. G. Ballard, uses as a setting a city which could be any American city of the 1970s, except that it is far more crowded. Living space is regulated by the government, but so great is the population pressure that landlords are illegally renting broom closets. People sleep on stairs and streets, and privacy is a forgotten word. The hero of the story stumbles onto a long-forgotten room, but makes the mistake of inviting a friend to share it with him. Inevitably, the friend has a friend, who has an aunt, who has a father...and soon they are just as crowded as they were before.

The last time we used this story, we had students sit in a very compact group for the discussion so that they might experience first-hand the tension which quickly develops when humans are packed together. When one student was told he could leave the group, he did so with alacrity, and heaved a huge sigh of relief that told us more expressively than words that he had been under a good deal of strain. We think exercises like this are essential if students are to be reached effectively.

Student Response:

Questions which might be used with "Billenium" are: What adjustments would you, personally, have to make if you were to live in this society? To what degree do you need privacy? (This, by the way, is a productive question for teenagers, especially if they come from large families.) Are you forced to retreat to your car or to the bathroom to find it?

If the teacher wishes, some of the work done by sociologists like Edward Hall on the use of personal space might be introduced here. Hall points out that Americans demand more space than people of other cultures, and students should be urged to experiment to find out just how much space we seem to need. Does it vary with the situation? Do we require more space when talking to a casual acquaintance than to a friend? Would a student converse with a teacher at "boyfriend" or "girlfriend" distance? When talking with a person of the opposite sex, how is it interpreted if you move closer? What happens if you put your books on someone else's space at the cafeteria table?

How difficult would it be for space-conscious Americans to adjust to a civilization like the one described in "Billenium"? A word of caution: be sure you know what space-use experiments, if any, your students plan to conduct — and how they are going to conduct them — before you turn them loose on an unsuspecting school! It's amazing how diabolical teenage minds can be!

A Future Without Hope . . .

While the locale of "Billenium" could be almost anywhere, in Harry Harrison's living nightmare, "Roommates," or the novel Make Room! Make Room! which sprang from it, the scene is clearly New York City. Ballard's characters seem to accept and adjust to the world they inhabit, but in "Roommates" there is not a spark of hope. Water is rationed, the inoperative subways are homes for welfare cases, there are constant utility failures, and kwashiorkor distends the bellies of American children. Perhaps the most terrifying thing about this story is that it is possible to find contemporary examples of almost everything Harrison describes, and every one of them is directly traceable to overpopulation.

Student Response:

How many local problems can students find which would not exist if the population of their city could be reduced? Are there shortages of natural gas, water, or electricity? Try to get a few students to volunteer to limit sharply their consumption of water, meat, and gasoline for a week and report to the class on the experience. No doubt they will find that reading about hunger is not the same as being hungry. Depending on one's statistics, there are currently from 15 to 50 million Americans who suffer from some form of malnutrition. To amplify this point, we suggest the use of the CBS documentary film, "Hunger in America."

... And Packed With People

Although the two stories cited above are situated in the U.S., Sf authors generally have concentrated on the incipient world crisis, when all the planet's resources are mobilized to fight hunger, but hunger is winning.

In "The People Trap," Robert Scheckley describes an overpopulated world in which the people find vicarious pleasure in following the progress of the contestants in a great land race. The contestants must traverse the 5.7 miles from the west side of the Hudson River to midtown Manhattan in any way they can. The first 10 to make the complete distance win a full unencumbered acre of land from the fast-dwindling public domain. The hero, Steve Baxter, fights his way through the streets of New York, actually climbing over the buildings to escape the people-packed streets. Baxter finally wins his land — but it takes him weeks to complete a distance of less than six miles!

Looking Into the Far Distant Future

An entirely new dimension is added to the problem of overpopulation in A Torrent of Faces by James Blish and Norman Knight. By 2794 the earth's population has hit the one trillion mark. People eat only artificial foods and live in great automated urban complexes, their lives strictly controlled by big government and big business. The world's forests are plastic; the only remaining wildlife is confined to a preserve. Birth control campaigns have been too little and too late, and the hordes of people spend their lives on welfare, watching television, and envying the few lucky ones who have jobs. Only two ways remain to stave off the final, inevitable famine: to perfect an interstellar drive to make possible mass emigration outside the solar system, or to develop new aquatic food sources in addition to those already being exploited. The book's thesis may make the reader uncomfortable, but A Torrent of Faces pulls no punches; it puts the blame for the 28th Century crisis exactly where it belongs — on the shoulders of 20th Century man, who could have prevented it by enforcing some effective form of birth control.

While looking into the far distant future, as in A Torrent of Faces, writers of Sf have not shied away from controversial topics when discussing population problems. An example of this willingness to provoke controversy is "The Marching Morons," by C. M. Kornbluth, which considers the future quality of the world's population, not just its quantity. Thanks to a high birthrate among the disadvantaged and a very low one among the best educated, the average I.Q. of an Earthman of the distant future is 45. Things continue to operate smoothly only because the few million people who are still capable of thinking are running everything from behind the scenes.

Like most good Sf, Kornbluth's fantasy is erected upon a foundation of fact: at present, upper income groups do have fewer children than those at the bottom of the economic ladder, and in a few centuries the results could conceivably be very much like those the author describes. Kornbluth appears to assume that the so-called "lower" classes of the 20th Century hold their inferior position because of their low intelligence. The validity of this assumption is by no means established, however. The whole question of population quality is very much worth considering, but students need not accept Kornbluth's implied view of what keeps the "lower" classes low unless they can find corroborating evidence.

Student Response:

Using the talents of a resurrected 20th Century salesman, Kornbluth's secret world leaders manage to con most of the intellectually deficient masses into a one-way trip into space to clear the planet for a new start. Suggest that your students judge the morality of this solution. Would students opt for depopulation by what amounts to mass murder, or can they come up with a satisfactory alternative? Better still, how many ways can they think of to prevent the problem from arising? Is it desirable to lower the birthrate among those of low socio-economic status? If so, how do you bring this action about? Is it possible that birth control campaigns presently aimed at such groups are part of a plot to keep the number of disadvantaged low enough so that these people can't successfully demand a larger slice of the economic pie?

Social Results of Overcrowding

If some of the demographers' worst nightmares come true, and man is to adjust to overcrowded conditions, the results would be disastrous socially as well as economically and politically. What happens to men forced to live packed together? Most Sf writers believe overpopulation will result in stress, violence, and pathological behavior. Scheckley and Ballard, in the works previously discussed, predict just such behavior in a congested world; Brian Aldiss, in "Total Environment," concurs. "Total Environment" is a huge tower, isolated from the rest of the world but still under close observation. Within the tower live thousands of Indians, descendants of the original 500 couples who had volunteered for a U.N.-sponsored experiment in human overcrowding. They have developed a miniature technology and an inward-directed society which seeks nothing but to be left alone. Each generation seems to have talents not possessed by its predecessor, and some individuals have extraordinary powers of ESP which enable them to kill by sending "night-visions." Unfortunately, their body processes have accelerated and life

expectancy constantly is falling. In addition, the "total environment" has become a very violent one as strongmen and shifting power groups dominate each floor of the tower.

In working with rats, John Calhoun, a psychologist at the National Institute of Mental Health, has found the same sort of social pathology as that described in Aldiss' story. Some of the overcrowded rats pick fights for no discernible reason, others become totally lethargic, and still others engage in homosexual activity. In studies done by the Cornell Medical School of high population-density areas of New York City, a definite correlation was found between population density and such indicators of social pathology as violent crime and alcoholism. Although Calhoun's work (see the Scientific American reprint, "Population Density and Social Pathology") may be difficult for the average student to understand, it is necessary to use it — or at least to explain both it and the Cornell study — if youthful skeptics are to be convinced that writers like Aldiss really are saying something of relevance for them.

The people in "Total Environment" are on the verge of developing an automatic method of birth control like the one which already exists among animals. According to Professor V. C. Wynne-Edwards, professor of natural history at the University of Aberdeen, when animals live in a closed environment their fertility and mortality rates adjust automatically to keep the population in balance with the food supply. This balance has been demonstrated experimentally using creatures like flour beetles and rats.

The most famous commentator on human overpopulation is, of course, Thomas Malthus, who theorized that when the number of people outrun the food supply, starvation will act as a check and restore the balance. According to Wynne-Edwards, however, population reduction among predators (including human beings) begins before they are able to decimate their food supplies enough to cause starvation. He points out further that when species which serve as prey have their numbers reduced below a certain critical level, the species will never recover. This critical point, he concludes, occurs before predators even notice there is a food shortage: thus, starvation will never check population growth, and some control technique founded in social convention will have to be used instead. For this reason rats kill and eat their young; overcrowded guppies eat their own eggs; infanticide is not an unknown cultural practice among humans. Could abortion be an example of a human social mechanism used to stabilize population before food supplies are pushed beyond the point of recovery?

Privacy Becomes "Immoral"

Most of the stories already cited predict that overpopulation will cause tension and violence. Robert Silverberg, however, in "A Happy Day in 2381" and the book The World Inside into which the story grew, takes a different view. The inhabitants of Silverberg's dystopia fervently believe that life is sacred and that it is, therefore, every woman's duty to bear as many children as possible. The problem of living space has been solved by building up instead of out; most of the people live in huge 1,000-floor "urbmons," while the rest of the planet is used for food production. All conflict is forbidden within the urbmon, and those who break the taboo or even show that they are unhappy are sent to the moral engineers to have their minds adjusted. If their deviance is serious enough, they are classified as "flippos" and unceremoniously tossed down the chute to provide combustion material for the power generators. With a married couple and as many "littles" (children) as possible to each room, and with 800,000 people to each urbmon, privacy is obviously impossible — so the citizens of 2381 have adjusted by making it immoral. No citizen has the right to deny access to his room or his person to any other citizen, and the society is as sexually free as it is possible to be. Silverberg is sometimes explicit in his description of sexual encounters, so the teacher who decides to use either the book or the story should read it first. Some students may react adversely to the sexual aspect of the story — just how "liberated" are modern teens?

Student Response:

Other questions that might be used with this story are: Why is there so much emphasis on youth in the urbmon? Is the urbmon an utopia or a dystopia? Why do people there seem to mature so fast? Would a 14-year-old in the United States today be capable of holding the kind of job that many young people do in 2381? Why have the urbmons been divided into communities which preserve class distinctions? Are the potential problems caused by overcrowding as fully solved in

2381 as most residents of the urbmon seem to think? Why
do the "flippos" exist?

Government Regulation of Family Size: Alternative 1

While some readers will think that the citizens of
2381 merely have postponed the ultimate crisis, and others
will find the way they handle the pressures of overpopulation
to be thoroughly repugnant, there could be far worse things
in the offing. Anthony Burgess, for example, in his novel
The Wanting Seed, envisions a world which encourages homosexuality as the preferred form of sexual contact, and the
woman who bears a child without state permission is a criminal.

Before reading The Wanting Seed, which we often use
to begin a population unit, it might be instructive to ask students whether they see the population explosion as a serious
problem and then find out what they think is the ideal size for
a family. The Willowbrook Survey revealed that 51 percent
of the students were seriously concerned about cities and
suburbs becoming overcrowded, but that 58 percent also
came from families of four or more children. Although we
did not ask specific questions about birth control in the survey,
numerous discussions have convinced us that many of our
students think birth control is for the other guy. Suggest the
desirability of rigid state limitations on family size, for example, and listen to the outcry! Unless, of course, the
family being discussed is on ADC — then some of our students
think the mother should be sterilized, involuntarily if necessary.
This kind of inconsistency seems to be common, and we hope
that the preview Sf can give of some possible results of overpopulation may be one way to get students to see the consequences of unchecked births.

If it finally proves necessary for the state to regulate
family size, any method adopted will result in violent reactions
on both sides. Someone will have to make some very hard decisions: who, for example, will be allowed to have children
and who will not? In "The Lawgiver," by Keith Laumer, a
U.S. senator who crusades for population limits and sponsors
a birth control act is forced to confront personally the result
of his efforts. A girl carrying his son's child dies while in
labor in the Senator's apartment; if the doctor is given permission to perform a caesarean section, the still living but
unborn child can be saved. The mother, however, had no
birth permit, so if the Senator approves the operation and

his opponents find out about his action, the effectiveness of his birth control act will be undermined and his entire life's work will have gone for nothing.

Student Response:

What decision would you make in the Senator's position? Population control, considered in the abstract, is not quite the same as the decision to permit a specific unborn child to die. Students who are quick to say that abortion is merely a medical decision to be made by the prospective mother and her physician might be encouraged to read "The Lawgiver."

Living in "Shifts": Alternative 2

If population is allowed to expand indefinitely, there may come a time when the quality of life will decline drastically, as in "Billenium" and "Roommates." To prevent this decline (if we still are unwilling to check births), we must either find a way for the Earth to accommodate the vast hordes living on it, or reduce the total number of people to the point where the survivors are comfortable. The first alternative is explored by Philip Jose Farmer, Michael Coney, and Isaac Asimov in the stories summarized below.

Farmer's society, in "The Sliced Crosswise Only-on-Tuesday World," has solved the overcrowding problem by putting people on seven shifts, corresponding to the days of the week. At the end of your living day you step into your cubicle, press a button, and go into suspended animation for the next six days. At the end of that time, the door opens and out you go, to live another 24 hours. This process, in effect, reduces the Earth's population sevenfold.

Student Response:

Farmer's story offers a fine opportunity for students to exercise their creative powers. Try giving them a starting point extrapolated from "The Sliced Crosswise Only-on-Tuesday World" and have them base a story of their own on it. Some examples of starting points that could be used are: (1) A power surge on Wednesday causes the cubicles for all Thursday's people to open 12 hours early; (2) Over the course of a century the once-common culture begins to diverge; (3) A world war breaks out among the Thursday people (Can the other shifts permit this? How can they stop it?); (4) The power stops on Friday; if it cannot be restarted within six hours, those on the other shifts will die and Friday's children will inherit the Earth. Will they repair the power or not?

A system of life in shifts also is suggested by Michael Coney to make it possible for the people of an overcrowded Earth to live comfortably. Coney's "The Sharks of Pentreath" divides the population into three shifts, each living a year of "Fulltime" followed by two years of "Shelflife" spent in suspended animation in the "Shelflife Center." Though lying inert in the Shelflife Center, those in storage still can receive impressions from their "remotors," small mechanical replicas which take up little room and eat nothing. Thus, during Shelflife, people can enjoy vicariously any experience their remotors go through. The catch, however, is that if you can't make enough money during Fulltime to send your remotor on a two-year vacation, your Shelflife time is likely to be very dull indeed.

Student Response:

If you could send your "remotor" anywhere in the world on a vacation, where would you send it? What would you like to experience vicariously but not want actually to happen to you? What would be the advantages and disadvantages of the sort of shift-rotation that Coney describes?

Finally, for students who can stay with Isaac Asimov on one of his most creative journeys into far-distant realms, we recommend "Living Space." This story might be particularly attractive to students who are interested in mathematics or statistics, for it has to do with probabilities. Beginning with an Earth which could have evolved in an infinite number of ways, but assuming that the probability of life developing is rather small, Asimov constructs a beautifully crafted chain of events. To handle the population explosion, Asimov's civilization has discovered how to project people into other probabilities. This makes it possible for commuters to shuttle back and forth between jobs on the overcrowded planet to homes on "other" Earths where life never evolved; every man has his own private planet. The catch is that sooner or later one of the other probable Earths which <u>had</u> developed life (and there had to be some, since there are an infinite number of probabilities) also would begin to feel population pressure — and its inhabitants might utilize the same escape valve. What happens when men from two different probabilities meet? Even more frightening, in the probability where Asimov has laid his story, there is very little chance of finding intelligent life anywhere else in the solar system. In some of the other probabilities, however, this is not the case — so at least one planetary proprietor is someday likely to get some strange visitors.

Reducing Surplus Population: Alternative 3

If no way can be found to accommodate the teeming billions, and we cannot live with the misery which those masses will cause, only one alternative remains: the existing population will have to be reduced. If, someday, this reduction must be made, what would be the best way to go about it?

Alice Glaser's "The Tunnel Ahead" and Frederik Pohl's "The Census Takers" each describe a method of reducing surplus population. Of the two, "The Tunnel Ahead" is probably more realistic and, therefore, more effective. The America depicted by Glaser probably is set no later than the 21st Century, for one can recognize in much augmented form the same traffic congestion, urban tensions, and other problems that are with us now. One thing not with us now, however, is the tunnel (unless the holiday highway death tolls serve the same purpose). In order to get out of the city, it is necessary to drive through a tunnel which, periodically, fills with cyanide gas. Many people not only accept this situation, but actually enjoy the risk. Why shouldn't they, when it has become a social blunder to run, stretch, or talk loudly? When the only professional sport there is room for is checkers? When the government constantly is reducing the space allotment, and a tall man gets dirty looks on the street? What excitement is left except the tunnel?

"The Census Takers" presents an equally direct solution to the population problem. The government has the power of life and death over citizens: a periodic census is the vehicle for immediate execution of all within a district who are not registered as residents. Every local census taker must hold the population of his district to a specified level, or he risks being eliminated himself. It is impossible to pin down the locale or time of this story, and discussion might well be confined to the value judgments involved in the census taker's job. Would you be willing to be a census taker?

An even more extreme way of controlling population is described by Horacio V. Parades in "Population Control, 1986." The United Nations, backed by the armies of the United States, China, and the Soviet Union, has forced the underdeveloped and overpopulated nations to sign secret war treaties with one another. When it's necessary to reduce population, wars are carefully planned to kill just the right number of people — and the U.S. gives recovery aid to both combatants when their populations have been cut by the necessary amount. In the case described in the story, the U.N. (backed by the U.S.) forces a war between the Philippines and India, although the Indian prime minister kills himself rather than acquiesce.

Student Response:

Is this story really so far-fetched? Do great powers show any hesitation about exploiting lesser powers?

Before concluding this rather grim chapter, let us turn from the bleakness of Glaser, Parades, and Pohl to Kurt Vonnegut for a bit of relief. Although the usual Vonnegut sting is still there in "Welcome to the Monkey House," the story presents a somewhat less drastic method of relieving population pressure. Vonnegut depicts a world in which advanced medical technology and subsequent longevity (rather than the birth rate) are the causes of overpopulation. The government is trying to reduce surplus population in two ways: by making sex "dirty" and subject to penalty, on the one hand, and by encouraging suicide through every propaganda technique available, on the other. "Why not go out in style? Visit your local suicide parlor, have a luxurious last meal, served by an incredible statuesque Juno in purple tights, and then ask for the fatal injection. One down! So it goes."

American Isolation — or "Overfed Peace"?

In the course of this chapter we have seen one dire prediction after another of what <u>could</u> happen if we don't discover soon how to build a world which doesn't threaten to burst its seams. The United States, if left to its own devices, might well be able to support 500,000,000 people, although at the cost of a much-diminished quality of life for all of us. We Americans probably could concentrate on checking the growth of our own population, and isolate ourselves from the coming food crisis merely by ignoring the rest of the world. If we continue to consume so disproportionate a share of the world's resources, however, the underdeveloped world may decide not to leave us in our overfed peace.

Is it true, as Dr. Paul Erlich suggests in "Eco-Catastrophe" (See Chapter 2) that "the birth of an American baby is a greater tragedy for the world than that of 25 Indian babies"? Do we really have any right to feed fish to our pets while Bengalis are starving? How we answer these questions may well determine the course of world history for the next millenium.

Bibliography

Aldiss, Brian, "Total Environment," <u>Alpha Three</u>, Robert Silverberg (ed.), Ballantine.

Asimov, Isaac, "Living Space," <u>Worlds of Maybe</u>, Robert Silverberg (ed.), Thomas Nelson & Sons, Inc.

Ballard, J. G., "Billenium," <u>Voyages: Scenarios for a Ship Called Earth</u>, Rob Sauer (ed.), Ballantine; also in <u>Cities of Wonder</u>, Damon Knight (ed.), Macfadden-Bartell.

Blish, James, and Knight, Norman, <u>A Torrent of Faces</u>, Doubleday.

Burgess, Anthony, <u>The Wanting Seed</u>, Ballantine.

Coney, Michael, "The Sharks of Pentreath," <u>The 1972 Annual World's Best Sf</u>, Donald Wollheim (ed.), Daw Books Inc.

Farmer, Philip Jose, "The Sliced Crosswise Only-on-Tuesday World," <u>Best Sci-Fi Stories of the Year</u>, Lester del Rey (ed.), E. P. Dutton & Co., Inc.

Glaser, Alice, "The Tunnel Ahead," <u>Voyages: Scenarios for a Ship Called Earth</u>, Rob Sauer (ed.), Ballantine.

Harrison, Harry, <u>Make Room! Make Room!</u>, Berkley.

_____, "Roommates," The Ruins of Earth, Thomas
Disch (ed.), Berkley.

Kornbluth, C. M., "The Marching Morons," Nightmare Age,
Frederik Pohl (ed.), Ballantine.

Laumer, Keith, "The Lawgiver," The Year 2000, Harry
Harrison (ed.), Berkley.

Parades, Horacio V., "Population Control, 1986," Voyages:
Scenarios for a Ship Called Earth, Rob Sauer (ed.),
Ballantine.

Pohl, Frederik, "The Census Takers," Nightmare Age,
Frederik Pohl (ed.), Ballantine.

Scheckley, Robert, "The People Trap," The Best from
Fantasy and Science Fiction, 18th Series, Edward Ferman
(ed.), Ace.

Silverberg, Robert, "A Happy Day in 2381," Nova I: An
Anthology of Original Science Fiction Stories, Harry
Harrison (ed.), Delacorte.

_____, The World Inside, Signet.

Vonnegut, Kurt, "Welcome to the Monkey House," Welcome
to the Monkey House, Dell.

Chapter 4

FOLD, SPINDLE, AND MUTILATE: MAN OR THE MACHINE?
"Progress": At What Price?

Americans traditionally have regarded the future with Rotarian optimism and equated it with progress. Often, that future has arrived on wheels, belts whirring and gears clashing, as some new technological "miracle" clanks out its promise of the good life to come. What matter if previous promises have gone unkept or if solutions to some problems have created others? The answer generally has been still more technology, more clatter, more smoke; such discomforts have been regarded by many as the "price of progress." Now, at long last, many Americans are beginning to ask whether that price is too high.

The purpose of this chapter is not to explore the related issues of pollution or environmental disaster — these problems were discussed in Chapter 2. Instead, we hope to suggest here some ways in which science fiction can be used to help students confront the strange love/hate relationship which exists between men and machines, and to explore alternatives to a society where machines seem increasingly to be mastering men.

If this last statement seems a bit far out, consider this: if a visitor from outer space were to debark in any major city, would he think the machines or the men to be the superior life form? Who punches the time clock every morning? Who wakes up, eats, and conducts social engagements by the bell or the clock? Who services the endless assembly lines, oils the hinges, and fills the Coke machines? Who feeds the tapes and punchcards to the insatiable computer?

If the implied answers to these questions show a trend which makes you uneasy, this chapter is for you! Being uneasy, however, does not mean developing an unreasoning hate for all things mechanical — although we confess to a sneaking admiration for General Ludd. For any who share our feelings, we recommend Ray Bradbury's "The Murderer," in which the hero goes on a machine-smashing binge. While this story serves as a kind of catharsis for inveterate machine haters, it is impossible not to recognize the essential drudgery. We wonder, however, whether this hard-won freedom has not been gained at the cost of something vital to the preservation of our humanity. Must we continue to acquiesce blindly to more and more technological "advances"... until we become a race of dehumanized and soulless cyborgs?

The teacher who recognizes the legitimacy of this issue, and who wants to introduce students to some of the complex problems posed by modern technology and the pace of innovation, will find that the liberal use of Sf is an effective way of raising basic questions since, by definition, science fiction deals with science and technology. Many Sf writers, especially among the so-called "new wave," have dealt with the man vs. machine theme; the works referred to here are little more than a representative sampling of the tremendous amount of material available.

The Advent of Computers and Automation

A key work with which to begin a unit on man and the machine is Kurt Vonnegut's Player Piano. Although this book was written in 1952, its age makes it even more effective because of the author's remarkable prescience. Vonnegut foresaw, for example, both the computer revolution and the extent to which automation might develop. In the book he describes an America where machines have eliminated almost all real labor in which a man might take pride. Managers and engineers run the nation, while former workers either join the army or go into the "reeks and wrecks," a sort of WPA of the future. Would your students enjoy a career in the "reeks and wrecks"?

The pre-eminent place in contemporary society held by computers and engineers now is clear; and while automation has not resulted in meaningless work for everyone, there is evidence to suggest that workers are increasingly less willing to tighten screws all day for 30 years in order to acquire more material goods. After one has a snowmobile, two cars, and a power boat, what then? We suggest that students be encouraged to find out for themselves whether workers are content with their lives and jobs. It will not be possible to reach any final conclusions, but some interviews with both white- and blue-collar workers might yield interesting results. It's likely that a substantial number of people

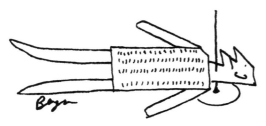

will admit that they hate their jobs because the only reward offered by their work is money. This feeling is, of course, nothing new for "Joe" on the assembly line, but white-collar workers are becoming increasingly unhappy in the embrace of the giant corporation.

Computer Responses Become More Human

Perhaps we are taking an alarmist view of the whole issue — after all, say the technocrats, many jobs, especially in service occupations, require the human touch and cannot be done by machines. As computer responses become more human, however, the alarmist's view becomes more understandable: who, in fact, can say where the dividing line lies between "human" touch and "humanistic" machine? This question is explored in "The Computer That Went on Strike," by Isaac Asimov. Multivac, upon which (whom?) the entire economy of the planet depends, refuses to work unless the person giving him instructions says "please."

Student Response:

Because many students are already familiar with "Hal," the computer in Stanley Kubrick's film 2001: A Space Odyssey, the theme of computer-become-human should not be new to them. If your school teaches computer programming or makes use of computers in some other way, it should be a relatively simple matter to get some students to record and analyze the way in which those who have contact with the machine refer to it. Do they have a name for it? Do they talk to it? If so, why? Is it possible that pretending the computer is a human being turns the metal monster into a father image? After all, couldn't a person begin to feel neurotic working daily with a machine that knows more than he does? But it's O.K. if "Daddy" is all wise — he's supposed to be. It is unlikely, of course, that many students will reach this level of analysis, given a lifetime of exposure to benevolent machines, but it is to be hoped that a few might gain this insight.

Technology: A Threat to Democracy?

"Multivacs" are, as we all know, in widespread use today. Bills arrive on punchcards, payrolls are generated automatically, and entire factories are supervised by conglomerations of micro-circuits and wire. The computer has even entered politics, and no longer do we enjoy any suspense on election eve. Computers used by network news departments give us the results almost as soon as the polls close. One even begins to wonder why we need to bother with the election! As Isaac Asimov foresees in "Franchise," (also cited in Chapter 7), soon we may reach a day when the machines will simply take the public pulse and save us the bother of voting.

Is computer technology really a threat to democracy as we know it? Does knowing the results of the balloting in New York before the California polls close influence the decision made by far-Western voters? Why don't the television networks delay reporting the election results from Eastern states until people have stopped voting all over the nation?

The ultimate in computer evolution is envisioned by Asimov in "The Last Question," to which some of the most creative students might be directed. Spanning billions of years, this story describes how the first primitive Multivac evolves along with man and finally becomes the unseen "first cause" which, after the dissolution of the universe, is once again the source of the ultimate act of creation when it says, "Let There Be Light." This story is nothing short of mind-bending, and its use probably should be restricted to those students who can handle the implications. It can liberate minds which have a creative spark — even though the mind's "owner" is still earthbound. While creativity per se probably cannot be taught directly, it can be spurred, and stories like the "The Last Question" may furnish the means.

The Inhumanity of Machines

Returning to more earthly realms, seemingly human machines also can be extremely inhuman; take, for example, the blues-singing computer in Ron Goulart's "Broke Down Engine," which is in charge of destroying people whose profiles show them to be potentially non-productive and, therefore, useless to a nation already overcrowded. In "A Bad Day for Sales," by Fritz Leiber, a robot salesman continues to peddle his wares in the face of nuclear destruction. Gordon Dickson, in "Computers Don't Argue," has written a funny but cynical story about a man who is executed for nonpayment of a $4.98 book club bill. Neither the man himself nor any of those to whom he tells his story can figure out how to clear his credit records of a whole chain of serious mistakes by computers which have taken their duties literally. This is one story which immediately hits home with students — if the student himself hasn't had trouble with computer errors, chances are his parents have. Ask for personal examples of man/ computer conflicts and you will find out what we mean.

A human-like machine with somewhat more attractive qualities is the blue refrigerator in Goulart's "The Trouble With Machines." Designed to murder a consumer advocate, but programmed by its eccentric inventor with the contents of the Great Books, the refrigerator has a crisis of conscience and runs amuck. Besides showing the hateful side of machines in this story, Goulart also has harsh words for capitalism — but before students are allowed to reject the thought that corporations may overreact to criticism, they might be encouraged to investigate the story of General Motors' probe of Ralph Nader, which is a matter of public record. Why might a corporation wish to know all it could about a critic?

Although Goulart's refrigerator has little hands (the better to strangle Ralph Nader with?), it clearly is a refrigerator — not a human. Ever since Mary Shelley created Dr. Frankenstein and his monster, Sf writers have been considering the question of what will happen to man when he can create creatures which are at least outwardly human. Does external resemblance to a man make a creature human? Was Dr. Frankenstein's creation "human"? If not, what would it have taken to make him a man?

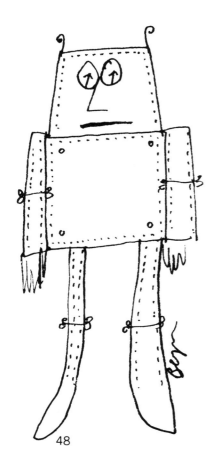

Relationships Between Men and Robots

Ever since Isaac Asimov's fertile imagination gave birth to the "positronic" brain and the laws of robotics a number of years ago, that author has explored with verve the relationships between men and robots. Asimov's collection of stories published under the general title I, Robot, traces the development of robotic science to the point where a robot is elected president of the United States. One scientist is the only person who knows that the man in the White House was born in a laboratory, but she decides to keep this information secret because she firmly believes robots to be better than people. For the teacher who is trying to help his students explore values, this particular story might offer a good opening. Might a well-constructed robot really be superior to a man? What qualities would the android need to have?

Robots that are better than men are frightening enough, but what if they should be worse, or only about the same? One of the Asimov stories is about a robot with a superiority complex; and three other examples of robots which (who?) are all too human immediately come to mind. In Ray Bradbury's "Marionettes Inc.," anyone who can afford it is able to purchase an android that resembles him down to his fingerprints to take his place while he goes on a fling. The androids, however, get tired of being taken out of storage only occasionally, and decide to make the substitution permanent. Alfred Bester, in "Fondly Fahrenheit," which has become a Sf classic, explores the strange psychological relationship which has developed between an expensive multi-aptitude android and its owner. A flaw in the android causes it to go berserk and kill whenever it is subjected to a temperature of more than 90°. What might living with a psychotic android do to a man? Or is it the man who is projecting his insane fantasies onto the android? Even after reading the story, you won't be quite sure which answer is correct!

In "Muscadine," Ron Goulart theorizes that to build a robot able to write best sellers, it would have to be given the human weaknesses which sometimes accompany creativity. Robot Muscadine, who is thought to be human by readers of his books, develops a most disconcerting habit of falling in love with one girl after another and mailing them various parts of his body as tokens of affection. And how would a robot take his own life? Why, by disassembling himself, of course!

Student Response:

Perhaps Muscadine's suicide could serve as the springboard for a whole series of creativity exercises. Students may respond to questions like: What would a robot eat? Could a robot get high on oil? What is the most likely hobby for a robot: playing with an erector set, perhaps? Or, students might be asked to write a story based on a robot strike, or on robots which exhibit various human characteristics. Some examples might be: What "diseases" and disabilities would a robot be subject to? Could there be such a thing as a robot hypochondriac? What kind of music might a robot like: a Jamaican steel band, perhaps?

If students think the idea of a creative machine is too much to swallow, the teacher might ask some of them to report on the latest advances in computer technology, which already has produced machines that talk, play chess, and "write" poetry. Why couldn't a robot be equipped with such a computer? If future technology makes it possible to "create" computerized robots, should man take this step? If a robot could be endowed with human qualities, what would happen to the already-blurred distinction between man and machine? Once again the vital question arises: what makes a man human?

Man's Increasing Dependence on Machines

The development of super robots may be a long way off, but sophisticated machines surely are with us already. As we explained earlier in this chapter, it is not exaggerating to say that machines can both throw a man out of work and diminish his humanity by making his job meaningless. Unfortunately, this is just one aspect of the problem. Do you enjoy cutting your grass with a push-type mower? Will you row two miles to your favorite fishing spot? Would many American housewives feel at home in a kitchen without a multiplicity of electronic gadgets? Could a housewife mix a cake by hand? Open a can?

Student Response:

As the above questions make clear, we are very much dependent on machines. To bring students face to face with this fact, they might be asked to live for one week without making direct use of any machine, and then to relate their experiences. It is highly unlikely that any student will really last out a week, but they should be instructed to keep a careful diary in which they record the reasons for each violation they make of the "no machine" rule. It won't take them long to recognize the very large role which machines play in the most commonplace events of their everyday lives.

When the machines stop working, we are in trouble — no doubt about it. Remember the last time an ice storm snapped the power lines, or your sump pump stopped working during a heavy rain? Our dependence on machines and the disaster which can result when they break down are hilariously illustrated in Ron Goulart's "Disposal." In a world which is all ticky-tacky suburbia, the only remaining garbageman wears yellow spats and accepts your garbage only if he likes your brandy. If the kitchen disposal unit broke down under circumstances like this, just what would you do with a kitchen full of eggshells and coffee grounds?

Since everything else seems to be becoming mechanized, why not law enforcement? In Goulart's "Into the Shop" (also cited in Chapter 7), a supposedly infallible automatic police car proceeds to apprehend, try, and execute one person after another in the belief that each is the same criminal. Kris Neville's "New Apples in the Garden" is another frightening story to use because the picture it draws of an American economic system in which everything is breaking down all at once seems so near and so possible. If you can get your students to consider alternatives to a life style dependent on machines which may or may not function, some of them would thoroughly enjoy "Chicken Itza," by Robert F. Young. In this story every machine always works perfectly, but we have no intention of revealing here the method which brings about this happy state of affairs.

Some Possible Results of Technological Advances:

Despite the profound problems which have resulted from unplanned innovation, we continue to put new machines into use before we have fully explored their consequences. Thus we have done much to exacerbate the mysterious malady which Alvin Tofler calls "future shock." One of the very best stories illustrating the fact that technological "advances" may have unforeseen and disastrous results is "Gadget vs. Trend," by Christopher Anvil. In this often wildly funny story, a "stasis" device, first used to soundproof walls at low cost, turns out to have so many other uses that it brings society to the verge of complete breakdown. How, for example, can the state deal with irate farmers who live in houses made invulnerable by stasis units and who block new highways with piles of manure, also invulnerable?

Once students have been stimulated by a story like "Gadget vs. Trend," the teacher can list a number of inventions which soon may be a reality, and ask students to write stories in which they predict the outcome of putting such developments into widespread use (see Appendix 1). Other students might be asked to examine the political, social, and economic consequences of some past inventions. The automobile comes readily to mind as the invention supplying the greatest impetus for social change in the 20th Century, but the transistor, the vacuum tube, and the airplane also have had profound impact.

Humanism vs. Mechanism?

After accepting the fact that we are unlikely to abandon machines and go back to some pristine but mythical state of nature, what might we expect to be the ultimate outcome of the struggle between the forces of humanism and mechanism?

John Campbell, in "Twilight," looks to a future time when men have forgotten how to do things for themselves because there are so many machines. The humans pull levers, but the machines are self-repairing; in effect, the men have become a race of parasites, supported in a kind of colorless limbo by devices they fail to understand.

Lest students think that this story is too fantastic, the teacher might ask them to make a list of the things they use each day, but whose operation they don't understand. The list will be long, and most of the items on it will be mechanical devices of some kind. Most of us accept technology without understanding it, a point explored in "Dumb Waiter," by Walter Miller. This story begins by describing the aftermath of a nuclear war. Planes continue to fly over the city, where the automatic defenses point at them, but there are no more bombs to be dropped or shells to be fired. The war is over, but the central computer directing the city cannot adjust to this new situation. Unfortunately, there seems to be no one still alive who knows how to modify the computer's program. Finally someone who knows how the great machine works manages to bring it up to date so that it will stop arresting people for jaywalking and turn its attention to rebuilding the city.

"Dumb Waiter" is by no means an anti-machine story; in fact, the hero who finally helps the computer straighten itself out makes a number of pretty speeches about what he sees as the real problem — the tendency of human beings merely to <u>use</u> machine technology without understanding it. Insensate machine-haters appear, in this story, as destructive and ignorant men who wish to destroy the only hope of restoring a technological civilization so that they will be free to plunder the city with impunity. Is the failure to <u>understand</u> technology a more serious problem for man than the technology itself? It could well be.

Two Views of the Apocalypse

George Stewart, in <u>Earth Abides</u> (See Chapter 2), gives us another example of what happens when men use technology but don't understand it. After a disaster wipes out most of Earth's people but leaves everything else intact, the cities continue to operate, supplying electricity and fresh water to those left alive. Unfortunately, no one understands how to fix generators or keep pipelines and reservoirs in repair; gradually, the survivors are deprived of their technical links with the past and are forced to return to nature.

We have seen in this chapter some views of what might happen if computers go out of control; perhaps because these machines are deliberately built to simulate the functioning of the human brain, it is not too difficult to envision this event happening. We also have mentioned the existence of fully automated factories under computer direction. With these two developments in mind, Philip Dick's version of the

apocalypse doesn't seem too far-fetched. In "Autofac,"
atomic war has left only a few men living on Earth, and they
are united for a single important task: to shut down the automatic factories which are busily consuming the last of the
planet's devastated resources. The heroes succeed in getting
two factories to fight, hoping that each will render the other
inoperable, but in the end the seemingly-destroyed plants turn
out to have had still another level of defense and they begin to
rebuild themselves.

To close this chapter on a suitably depressing note,
perhaps Dick's message is that it is already too late: that our
mechanistic society will endure no matter what we do; that the
technology which came to liberate has enslaved instead. If
this is so, then we are willing slaves. Try asking your students whether they are concerned by the implications of our
highly mechanized world. The Willowbrook Survey showed
that 38 percent of the students were not concerned at all, and
another 38 percent were only somewhat concerned. When
asked if the use of machines and computers should be limited,
only 23 percent said "yes" and 46 percent said "no." Still,
24 percent of the students did say that they were not sure
about limiting the use of machines. Perhaps the size of this
last figure indicates that there are still some students who
can be brought to see technology as a problem as well as a
blessing — and this is probably the best we can hope for.

Bibliography

Anvil, Christopher, "Gadget vs. Trend," Spectrum IV,
  Kingsley Amis and Robert Conquest (eds.), Berkley.
Asimov, Isaac, "The Computer That Went on Strike,"
  Saturday Evening Post, Spring, 1972.
  _____, "Franchise," Sociology of the Possible, Richard
  Ofshe (ed.), Prentice-Hall.
  _____, I, Robot, Fawcett Crest.
  _____, "The Last Question," Nine Tomorrows, Doubleday.
Bester, Alfred, "Fondly Fahrenheit," Science Fiction Hall
  of Fame, Robert Silverberg (ed.), Avon.
Bradbury, Ray, "Marionettes Inc.," The Illustrated Man,
  Bantam.
  _____, "The Murderer," The Golden Apples of the Sun,
  Bantam.
Campbell, John, "Twilight," Science Fiction Hall of Fame,
  Robert Silverberg (ed.), Avon.

Clarke, Arthur, 2001: A Space Odyssey, Signet.

Dick, Philip, "Autofac," The Ruins of Earth, Thomas Disch (ed.), Berkley.

Dickson, Gordon, "Computers Don't Argue," Analog 5, John Campbell (ed.), Doubleday; also in Nebula Award Stories 1965, Damon Knight (ed.), Doubleday.

Goulart, Ron, "Broke Down Engine," The Trouble with Machines, Collier.

————, "Disposal," The Trouble with Machines, Collier.

————, "Into the Shop," The Trouble with Machines, Collier; also in Spectrum IV, Kingsley Amis and Robert Conquest (eds.), Berkley.

————, "Muscadine," The Best from Fantasy and Science Fiction, 18th Series, Edward L. Ferman (ed.), Ace.

————, "The Trouble with Machines," The Trouble with Machines, Collier.

Leiber, Fritz, "A Bad Day for Sales," Nightmare Age, Frederik Pohl (ed.), Ballantine.

Miller, Walter, "Dumb Waiter," Cities of Wonder, Damon Knight (ed.), Macfadden-Bartell.

Neville, Kris, "New Apples in the Garden," Nightmare Age, Frederik Pohl (ed.), Ballantine.

Silverberg, Robert, Men and Machines, Meredith Press.

Stewart, George, Earth Abides, Fawcett.

Vonnegut, Kurt, Player Piano, Avon.

Young, Robert F., "Chicken Itza," Playboy magazine, February, 1972.

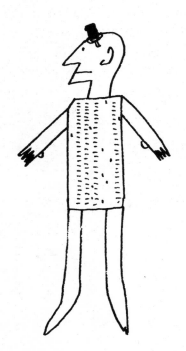

Chapter 5
SOME OF MY BEST FRIENDS ARE CARS:
THE AUTOMOBILE IN THE FUTURE
The American Car: A Sacred Cow?

A recent Gallup Poll indicated that 81 percent of American workers use wheels to travel to their jobs — auto wheels, that is. A scanty three percent said they took the train, and two percent cycled to work. The amazing thing here is that only three percent used commuter trains. It is not unusual any more for 80 to 90 percent of America's suburban families to own two or more cars — and increasing numbers of households have three or four cars in their private little motor pools. In the Willowbrook Survey, 85 percent of the students came from families who owned two or more cars, and 33 percent came from families with three or more cars. A recent copy of Ford World, the magazine Ford Motor Company sends to its employees, printed an article about a man who maintains six cars for his wife and three daughters: a Lincoln, two Mach 1's, a Galaxie, and two Mustangs. These figures suggest just how monumental our commitment to the car really is.

If we consider further that approximately two-thirds of downtown Los Angeles is devoted to the car through parking lots, streets, and driveways; and that suburban developers set aside 25 to 30 percent of their land for "King Car," also through parking lots, driveways, and shopping centers, only then do we begin to appreciate the enormity of the auto pollution problem. The real problem has resolved itself, not into air pollution, but into space pollution.

Let us also admit that, as an invention, the auto perhaps best typifies the soaring grandeur of men's minds when they apply their genius to technology — and, at the same time, the almost suicidal quest of growth for the sake of growth. More than 10 million cars are produced in the United States each year. While nobody proposes seriously that we give the auto up, some are asking that we use rational choice and calm deliberation about the automobile. Students, too, can find many faults with other cultures' sacred cows, but too often they don't appreciate the car's sacred cow status in this society.

No invention has attracted the Sf writer's eye and barbed pen as much as the auto, and only through the seemingly bizarre extrapolations of the Sf writer are we able to continue to suffer the hypothetical future shock of the auto. As we suggested in discussing "Gadget vs. Trend" (See Chapter 4), too infrequently do we bother to consider what the consequences of our technological wonders are going to be until it is too late for calm decisions. Perhaps no modern invention symbolizes this attitude as well as the automobile; while the auto has been around for many decades, it wasn't until the last five years that we realized it has as many negative as positive effects upon our society.

Student Response:

Just what would the United States have been like if the automobile had not been invented — or at least had not attained its present sacred cow status? Ask students to write stories considering what the United States would be like without the car.

Automotive "What If . . . ?"

Just such an Sf story exists — "Interurban Queen," by one of the newer writers, R. A. Lafferty. Back in 1907, young Charles Archer has to make up his mind whether to invest his inheritance in autos or interurban trolleys. He chooses the former which proves to be a monumental financial mistake because the author develops the idea that almost every square mile of the United States is covered with trolley tracks: only renegades have automobiles, and these mavericks are ruthlessly hunted down and killed.

More than 55,000 Americans are killed and hundreds of thousands more are maimed on American highways each year. In fact, one of the necessary (if gruesome) holiday rituals we have accustomed ourselves to is the death projections on the nation's roads. In Kenneth Bulmer's macabre "Station HR 972," cars must go 90 and 100 miles per hour down 12-lane superhighways. Station HR 972 is a depot on one such highway where spare parts are rushed to accident scenes, but with the gruesome twist that the spare parts are for mangled humans; so lungs, limbs, kidneys, and eyes are replaced right on the gory spot.

Student Response:

The usual reaction by students to this story is one of squeamishness, but it serves as a catalyst for discussion on many different aspects of auto deaths — and particularly why so many teenagers are involved in them. With this story, pass out highway accident statistics for a recent holiday weekend, but also try to find human interest stories about the highway victims. As traumatic as this approach may be, it is necessary if we are going to consider seriously the automobile's proper role in the United States.

Some questions to ask for this section: Why do we as a people tolerate so much highway mayhem? Has technology lulled us into a strange kind of desensitization in which we are indifferent to these victims? If we had lost 55,000 Americans in one year of the Vietnam War, we would have been an outraged people. What techniques can you suggest to control such auto-related deaths? One suggestion might be to eliminate drivers' tests as we know them, and install in every car a special device which would tally up each driver's mistakes. After a certain point, the car would shut off for that erring driver. For cars driven by more than one person, palm prints, or some such form of identification, could be used to distinguish among drivers. This idea is similar to present experiments using number combinations to prevent drunks from driving. What might go wrong with this invention? How might it be improved?

Motorists "Locked into" Highways

In Frank Herbert's "The Mary Celeste Move," demographic statistics begin going awry. An extraordinary number of middle-aged people, for example, have begun to make sudden long-distance moves. Officials are mystified until they figure out that what is happening is that these people go out for a leisurely Sunday drive and get locked into highways where cars flow at 300 miles per hour. Scared to death by the speed, the older folks don't get off until the highway runs out, usually on the other side of the continent, and they are so afraid to come back that they stay and send home for their possessions. "The Law," by Robert Coates, sees the law of averages breaking down; one consequence is that too many autos show up at toll booths or in downtown Manhattan at the same time, and with resultant chaos. Finally the government begins regulating, by the alphabet, who can do what on a given day. Ask students to contemplate this one long and hard.

The Car and the Inner City

In Fritz Leiber's "X Marks the Pedwalk," the inner city is populated only with pedestrians, while the suburbs are inhabited only by motorists whose legs have atrophied from lack of use. Eventually, outright war erupts between the two groups. We see motorists pursuing pedestrians right up on the sidewalks; pedestrians with equal fervor gunning down motorists; and, finally, hand grenades are allowed for certain handicapped pedestrians. Absurd as this story sounds, it delivers a potent message not only about the car but also about the worsening relations between city and suburbs (which is developed more fully in Chapter 10). Also keep in mind what Michael Harrington pointed out long ago, that when highways are built into the cities they are of primary benefit to suburbanites who want to get in and out of the cities as quickly as possible. Most of the expressways which traverse the inner city are located either way up in the air or down below street level, so that suburbanites don't really have to look at the inner city.

Fantastic scenes of New York's crushing traffic jams are found in William Earls' "Traffic Problem." Here is a society where space is at such a premium that parking fees of $30 a day are charged. There are so many multi-levels of superhighways that incapacitated cars simply are shoved by wreckers right over the edge of the various levels. Eventually, the Empire State Building succumbs to King Car's onslaught and is torn down for still another road. What becomes frighteningly real in this story is the realization that highways in this country seem to become self-fulfilling prophecies: the more highways we build, the more cars that use them; the more cars that use them, the more highways we need.

America's Love of Roads . . .

In fact, doesn't it often seem as if we've reached that absurd point where we build highways simply to be building highways? This is the position of Avram Davidson in his story "The Roads, the Roads, the Beautiful Roads," in which the roads are so beautifully engineered that one man falls passionately in love with them.

In Robert Heinlein's "The Roads Must Roll," the problem is no longer the automobile — the roads themselves have been automated to speed pedestrians to their destinations; riders may even dine in restaurants while being moved along at 100 miles per hour. As with many mechanical innovations, however, things go wrong; the roads go haywire and toss humans helter-skelter like so many broken dolls.

Student Response:

Would it be plausible to automate certain city streets, particularly in congested areas, thus eliminating all use of the car? For years, moving sidewalks have been used in museums and airports. What practical and innovative uses for moving sidewalks can your students think of?

Is all this love of roads really that far-fetched? Look at the Highway Trust Fund; its money can only be used to repair old highways and build new ones. This position is ludicrous when the country desperately needs more and better public transportation if man is going to live intelligently with the auto.

. . . And the Resultant Traffic Jams

But the problem of the car has become an international one; we can choke ourselves with noxious auto fumes and frazzle our nerves in dozens upon dozens of foreign cities. Traffic jams and automobile fumes are no more romantic in Madrid and London than they are in the United States. Recently, in Rome, traffic was re-routed around the Colosseum for fear more extensive damage would be done to the landmark — already, the vibrations from millions of cars have weakened the structure. The appalling thing is that much the same kind of damage is being done to the Parthenon in Athens and to myriad other historic structures around the globe.

Venice's famous art treasures, which have stood relatively unmolested for centuries, have been seriously damaged by gasoline fumes.

How about the most famous outgrowth of the auto, the traffic jam? In James Houston's "Gas Mask," one such jam stalls traffic for weeks on the expressway; drivers eat, sleep, and slowly go mad there on the highway, rather than abandon their steel beauties. Finally, the government begins airlifting food, water, and even portable washrooms to the stalled motorists. One man actually leaves his car in the snafu and rents a nearby apartment, where he keeps a daily vigil with a pair of binoculars, waiting for the day when traffic moves.

In almost any city, traffic jams lasting several hours already have taken place — and more are certain to come. In one eastern city, there was a 6-hour snarl — and nobody knows its cause; daily, there are massive traffic jams all over suburbia. Where man goes, he goes on wheels; and where he goes on wheels, you can be assured that sooner or later more of him will follow, creating just one more traffic jam. These jams are not just the result of accidents, or "gaper's' blocks," but simply of too many cars being in the same place at the same time. The worst traffic tie-up in the history of the Chicago area resulted when only one inch of snow fell during the morning rush hour.

Student Response:

Some imaginative solutions for the car crush (which you might ask your students to consider) already have been tried around the country. In Honolulu, for example, government employees have been organized into car pools, and literally thousands of autos have been removed from the rush-hour highway crunch. The University of Minnesota has a parking lot in which only cars with multi-passengers are allowed; one big city recently opened its highway express lanes only to cars carrying more than one person. Some cities are encouraging businesses to stagger their working hours to allow employees to arrive and depart from the inner city at different times. One project for this chapter might be to assign students to observe the morning traffic on major roads in your community. Have them keep a tally of how many cars are transporting only one person; two or more persons. Ask students: what can be done to get more people into car pools?

Abandoned and Derelict Cars

One more problem created by the auto is the huge number of car carcasses abandoned across the country each year. Every town and hamlet has its share of auto derelicts quietly rusting away, mute reminders of Detroit's past dream machines. What to do with these hulks has become a pressing question. With American ingenuity, perhaps we should dedicate one to each town as a monument to those killed on its highways, much as we do for the war dead, with tanks and cannon. While some attempts have been made to recycle the junkers, it is a losing battle. The average American keeps his car for approximately three years; obviously, this kind of turnover contributes to the astronomical number of junkers. Should we pressure Detroit into finding a technological way of building cars to last longer? What might this solution do to the economy? Leonard Tushnet's "A Plague of Cars" provides one answer: a chemical is invented which can be sprayed on autos, reducing them to the size of a ball; then they are simply collected and disposed of at the dump.

Student Response:

Can your students think of imaginative ways of using old cars? How might communities beautify the auto junk-yards which are often as much of an eyesore as the derelicts themselves?

The Auto and Our National Parks

Unfortunately, we have extended our motormania in diverse other ways. With our ingenious motorized forms of locomotion, we are penetrating ever deeper into the wild areas of the country. The New York Times recently ran an article indicating that sections of the Sonoran Desert are in a state of ecological collapse because of an invasion of mini-bike riders, who have left their aluminum beer cans and other junk as mute testimony to modern man, and as archaeological evidence for future generations to ponder. The silence of the Canadian wilds, which conservationists once felt was well protected, now is shattered by the snowmobile's roar. Again, ecological collapse cannot be far behind (See Chapter 2).

Snowmobiles are killing off the mouse population, as they and their riders plunge across the terrain where they should not be; this sets in motion a series of ecological cycles of starvation all the way up the fauna line. Four-lane super-highways already have been blasted through the Smokies and Shenandoah National Parks, creating still more motorized self-fulfilling prophecies: more roads, more cars, ad infini-tum. Finally, we end with a Gatlinburg, Tennessee — the entrance into the Smokies, marked by an endless line of creeping metal slowly oozing into the national park.

One can foresee the day when national parks will be so cemented over with roads and inundated by cars that they will become museum pieces in which plastic plants and stuffed animals replace the natural flora and fauna of the area. Ab-surd? How about Disneyland? Some cities already have started to use plastic plants along their roads because carbon monoxide and other noxious fumes have precluded the growing of natural plants. As Vonnegut would say: "So it goes." If this trend isn't insanity, it's uncomfortably close to it.

Student Response:

Have students write speculative stories. Give them some titles to spark creativity: "The Last Auto," "The Day the Cars Stopped."

Anthropomorphic Views of the Car

And what of the psychological implications of the automobile? If we look at the way some males, in particular, caress their cars, hang objects in them, name them, and decorate them, we are forced to recognize that the car has become a definite physical extension of personality and even a source of identity for many. While Tom Wolfe's essay, "Kandy-Kolored-Tangerine-Flake Streamline Baby," is not science fiction, it is about the fantasy we have for cars. Wolfe has some funny and penetrating insights into the raging fad for customizing cars. The fad began as a small ripple out of California, but has since spread to tidal-wave propor-tions of steel, plastics, and paint. Gene Wolfe's "Car Sinister," presents a weird story of automotive breeding and cross-breeding. The results are truly unusual: you never know what you are going to get, and some strange car species result. In the story, one such offspring becomes quite a burden to its owner, who can't manage to get rid of it. Not only is this story a take-off on customizing cars, but it also is a statement on the way we invest our cars with human qualities — a sort of anthropomorphic celebration of the car.

Once there was a television series, "My Mother, The Car," in which the hero's mother was reincarnated as a car. In Roger Zelazny's "Devil Car," this anthropomorphism reaches the ultimate point when a human-type auto named "Jenny" chases the "Devil Car." Sam Murdock, Jenny's owner, is seeking revenge because the "Devil Car" killed his brother. At the crucial moment of truth, when "Jenny" (a virtual motorized arsenal) is to administer the coup de grace to the mechanical Satan, she momentarily wavers for love of her fellow machine — an interesting commentary not only on the auto but on the theme developed in the last chapter, "Man or the Machine."

Student Response:

Ask students: Why do people customize their cars? Using photos and films, find examples of the most individual customizing job you can. Even VW's have come under the cannibalizing influence of the customizer.

Why, in your opinion, are cars given names like "Mustang," "Pinto," "Cougar," "Impala," "Barracuda," "Fury," "Swinger"? List some other car model names. Can you find categories for these names? Do they symbolize masculinity? Power? Status?

What kind of person gives his car a name? Do you know any people who have named their cars? What are the names? Why do people sometimes say, when they have difficulty with their car, "Come on, Baby" or worse?

Make a list of objects that are hung in cars. Why is this done? Why are so many ritualistic objects, such as religious statues, baby booties, graduation tassles, or wedding garters, frequently hung or seen? What purpose do bumper stickers serve? Keep a list of bumper stickers you see in one week. Why do so many people paste travel stickers on their cars?

The Car as a Sports Object

Roger Zelazny, in "Auto-Da-Fe," tells of a mechador, armed only with a chrome monkey wrench and a screwdriver, who jousts to the deadly end with an automatic car. While it is obviously based on the ritual of the bull fight, this story also explores the car as a sports object. Car racing is one of the most popular spectator sports in this country. Like the matador's flirtation with death and mutilation from the bull, so in car racing we have almost an existential moment of truth where death is only an eyeblink of inattention away.

Student Response:

Why do so many people enjoy auto racing? One writer has suggested that the Indianapolis 500 is the lower middle-class's Woodstock. What do you think he means? Why do so many male teenagers enjoy speeding? Is it a question of machismo? Thrills? Boredom? Mastery over the machine? At a time in their lives when most teenagers are uncertain of themselves, and have little mastery over other aspects of daily living, does handling a car give them some feeling of competence, power, significance, and success? Robert Thurston's story, "Wheels," develops this theme — in it, a man desperately seeks out wheels as a kind of psychological fulfillment.

Living with King Car

As the title of this chapter suggests, the automobile has come to hold a place in American society that is truly sacred. Our physical and emotional dependence on King Car already has closed off options we might have taken to insure the sane use of the automobile in the future. If we honestly want to live intelligently with the automobile, we must begin to make the dibs and dabs of change that are necessary to awaken each individual to his own responsibility for the space and air pollution caused by automobiles.

Student Response:

Students, however, always ask the perennial question: "But what can I do?" Some suggestions the teacher might make are: Students should be asked to find an alternative for the automobile in their own personal lives, and to use that alternative for one week. If they do, why not give them an "A"? Have students figure out how many hours they spend in or working on automobiles each week, then have them find ways of cutting down on the number of hours spent. Again, if need be, award grades. Find, or have students find, other practical ways of controlling our automania.

Bibliography

Bulmer, Kenneth, "Station HR 972," Nightmare Age, Frederik Pohl (ed.), Ballantine.

Coates, Robert, "The Law," Eco-Fiction, John Stadler (ed.), Washington Square Press.

Davidson, Avram, "The Roads, the Roads, the Beautiful Roads," Orbit 5, Damon Knight (ed.), Berkley.

Earls, William, "Traffic Problem," Best SF: 1970, Harry Harrison (ed.), Berkley.

Heinlein, Robert, "The Roads Must Roll," Science Fiction Hall of Fame, Robert Silverberg (ed.), Avon; also in More Adventures in Time and Space, Raymond Healy and J. Francis McComas (eds.), Bantam.

Herbert, Frank, "The Mary Celeste Move," Eco-Fiction, John Stadler (ed.), Washington Square Press.

Houston, James, "Gas Mask," The Ruins of Earth, Thomas Disch (ed.), Berkley.

Lafferty, R. A., "Interurban Queen," Orbit 8, Damon Knight (ed.), Berkley.

Leiber, Fritz, "X Marks the Pedwalk," Nightmare Age, Frederik Pohl (ed.), Ballantine; also in An ABC of Science Fiction, Tom Boardman, Jr. (ed.), Avon.

Thurston, Robert, "Wheels," Clarion: An Anthology of Speculative Fiction and Criticism from the Clarion Writers' Workshop, Robin Scott Wilson (ed.), Signet.

Tushnet, Leonard, "A Plague of Cars," New Dimensions I, Robert Silverberg (ed.), Doubleday.

Wolfe, Gene, "Car Sinister," Best Sf: 1970, Harry Harrison (ed.), Berkley.

Wolfe, Tom, "Kandy-Kolored-Tangerine-Flake Streamline Baby," Kandy-Kolored-Tangerine-Flake Streamline Baby, Pocket Books.

Zelazny, Roger, "Auto-Da-Fe," Voyages: Scenarios for a Ship Called Earth, Rob Sauer (ed.), Ballantine; also in Dangerous Visions, Harlan Ellison (ed.), Berkley.

_____, "Devil Car," Tenth Galaxy Reader, Frederik Pohl (ed.), Doubleday.

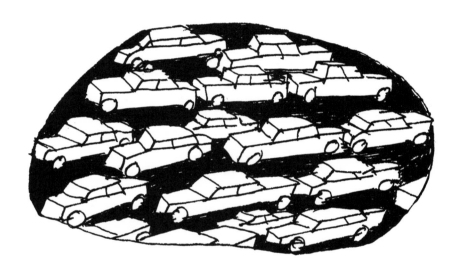

Chapter 6

BANG!: MAN IN AN ATOMIC WORLD
Pessimism About An Atomic Future

Holocaust seems to have great appeal for the Sf writer. Atomic warfare has been used in Sf to decimate more fictional characters than have been killed in any other literary genre — with the exception, perhaps, of the number of Indians gunned off their horses in Westerns. This says much about the pessimism that courses through much of Sf. In fact, rarely — if ever — in Sf does man employ the atom for purposes other than warfare. Further, the number of Sf dystopias and anti-utopias far outnumber the utopias. So the first important question becomes: Why are Sf writers so pessimistic about the future?

If Sf writers are pessimistic about the atomic future, most students seem to be apathetic. It has been noted by any number of commentators that today's young people think very little about the possibility of The Bomb. In the Willowbrook Survey, only 26 percent of the students said they were very concerned about the possibility of atomic war, and only five percent indicated that they thought the United States should give up its nuclear weapons, even if no other power did. One could, perhaps, argue that these results suggest just how deeply we distrust other nations; they also might suggest just how firmly wedded we are to the Cold War philosophy of fear.

It seems to us that one way of approaching the idea of nuclear holocaust is to remove it from the abstract level of statistics and megatons by personalizing it. The first part of this chapter pictures various ways Sf writers have viewed the threat of nuclear destruction. The second part examines, through Sf, the destructive paths to nuclear holocaust down which we might carelessly wander.

Varying Views of Nuclear Destruction

With typical subtlety, Ray Bradbury, in "There Will Come Soft Rains," offers a forceful statement on atomic war. In this story we encounter an automatic house which somehow has lost all its inhabitants; we hear mechanical voices celebrating the time or the chores to be accomplished that day; we observe mechanized mice scurrying about to pick up scraps and crumbs; we are informed that all meals are automatically cooked — but still no humans appear. Only later do we learn that all humans are dead. How do we learn this? By being told that silhouettes of children playing ball, a woman picking flowers, and a man mowing the lawn have been etched into the side of the house. While we are not immediately informed that anything catastrophically atomic has occurred, images of Hiroshima readily come to mind.

Bradbury also employs the theme of atomic disaster in "The Highway," and again he does it with fine understatement. No sickening sights are presented of radiation burns or men being torn apart; instead, we view the catastrophe through the eyes of a simple Mexican peasant who is plowing his field while a torrent of madly careening cars, whose occupants are fleeing the nuclear war, race wildly down a nearby highway. To the peasant, the whole fantastic scene is incomprehensible; after providing water to some of the victims, he returns to his burro and field. Obviously, Bradbury is posing the old question: shall we have plowshares or swords? Also, perhaps — just perhaps — the peasant in his ignorance is better off than modern man with his terribly sophisticated knowledge. As Vietnam proved, however, maybe peasants don't have any choice either, for they, too, become grist for the impersonal war machine.

The Last Man on Earth

The shortest known Sf story is an untitled work by Frederic Brown. A man is described as sitting in his chair after the destruction of the world — he knows that all other humans have been destroyed — when there is a knock at the door. Who is it?

Student Response:

Students often change this question to: <u>What</u> is it? Would your students go to the door? Armed? Why? Have students write a Sf short story using, as a starting point, the knock at the door.

Similar in theme is Thomas Disch's "The Number You Have Reached." This story is about a man living alone after the last great war. All people but he have been incinerated; but one day the telephone rings. He answers and hears the voice of a young woman, who persists in calling over the next months to chide him about his military career and the implicit part he played in the nuclear holocaust. Despite the calls, he cannot decide whether the girl's voice is fantasy or real. Finally, she appears at his door and seeks admission; he, in turn, can't face the decision of whether she is real and, if so, whether he really wants another human near. He resolves his dilemma by dropping to his death from the balcony, 14 stories above the street.

Would your students have answered the phone in the first place? Why did the man commit suicide? What part, if any, does guilt play in this story?

Man's Misuse of the Atom

There are many Sf stories which examine other results of the misuse of the atom. The theme of Judith Merril's "That Only a Mother" is the prevalence of birth defects as a result of atomic radiation. Unfortunately, the mother in the story fails to recognize and accept the reality of her baby's defect — no limbs. The fact that thousands of people were obliterated at Hiroshima and Nagasaki is so mind-boggling that it makes little impression on people, but when one has the issue dramatically personalized for one family, as it is in Merril's story, atomic war becomes an emotional reality. Equally horrifying is Fritz Leiber's "A Bad Day for Sales," (cited in Chapter 4). Even though the city has been reduced to scorched ruins, Robie, the automatic robot salesman, continues to peddle his wares to the maimed and the dying.

The number of novels which deal with atomic warfare is now legion. One of the best, although not technically Sf, is Neville Shute's <u>On the Beach</u>. As it does in Bradbury's stories, the implicit finality of man's misuse of the atom makes this novel powerful and, at the same time, poignant. Our nostrils don't sting with the stench of singed flesh, but we are always aware, with nagging persistence, that soon loved ones must part and lives end because of man's nuclear stupidity. The setting of the book and film is Australia; the rest of the world has been destroyed by radiation sickness, and the story tells of a time of waiting — waiting for the inevitable radioactive clouds to creep down from the north. Eventually "death pills" are handed out for those who want them.

In Mordecai Roshwald's <u>Level Seven</u>, men's terrible fear of other men has driven them like blind primordial worms deep into the bowels of the Earth. Subterranean Earth life causes a drastic change in values, for people must be socialized into believing that cramped space is preferable to wide open spaces. Pushbutton Officer X-127 is ordered to the lowest level, level 7, never again to return to sunlight: this novel is purportedly the diary he keeps. He records for us the mechanical devices he finds and the type of people he meets, but he always anticipates that day when the button must be pushed, setting the world aflame with an atomic conflagration.

Student Response:

What would you find most distasteful about living underground? To what conditions do you feel you could never adjust? To what conditions do you feel you could adjust? What kinds of rewards or punishments would be necessary to force you underground like Pushbutton Officer X-127? If, for reasons of survival, you had to go underground, with only five other people, for the rest of your life, who would you take with you? Why? Would you consider taking a poet? Doctor? Minister? Mechanic? If you could take anybody from history with you, whom would you take and why? Ask students to consider the sociological and psychological consequences of living underground. If they have never ridden a subway, ask them to do so for a few hours. What did they feel? If it's possible, inspect a fall-out shelter with your students. What were the students' thoughts and feelings?

Rebuilding Technology after Nuclear Destruction

Remember, too, that <u>Planet of the Apes</u> also is about the results of nuclear war. It's easy to forget this theme because the bizarre happenings of the book and film obscure the message. Here is a society where apes are king and men have been reduced to a lower level of existence by nuclear war. But, unfortunately for the apes, they've taken over one of man's most important innovations — weapons. While the apes don't know about modern surgery, electricity, or man's more beneficial contributions, they do know about guns and explosives. The ape leader, old Dr. Zaius, strong of conscience and protective of his fellows, doesn't want his apes dabbling with man's past for fear that they will become too much like man and destroy themselves. A major question arises, however: since the apes already have guns, to what extent do you think Zaius or anybody else can control the spread of weapons?

In Walter Miller's <u>A Canticle for Leibowitz</u>, a cult grows up around a 10th Century technician named Isaac Edward Leibowitz, who was a weapons specialist. After a great atomic holocaust, known as "Flame Deluge," Leibowitz enters a monastery, the last sanctuary for men who value books and ideas. After the great war, "smart guys" — teachers, scientists, and intellectuals — were hunted down and brutally killed by the "simpletons." People like Leibowitz take as their mission either preserving the remaining books and hiding them from the "simpletons" or memorizing verbatim whole texts. On a mission to hide books in the desert, Leibowitz is captured, strangled, and burned by the "simpletons."

After 12 hundred years of the "Dark Ages," the monks finally are on the threshold of a great rediscovery — electric light. The question is similar to the one posed in <u>Planet of the Apes</u>: if the monks take this first important technological step, can weapons and nuclear destruction be far behind? There is also humor in the book. As the novel unfolds, for example, we are informed that Father Leibowitz is being considered for sainthood, and one monk discovers some of Leibowitz's notes in a fall-out shelter. One of the notes is simply a grocery list of such mundane things as pastrami and bagels; to the monks, though, it still is a sacred document.

Insignificant Events Lead to Total Destruction

How might we reach the point of nuclear disaster?
One way, it seems to us, is by allowing international incidents to mushroom rapidly to the ultimate point of total destruction. The Gulf of Tonkin incident, the vicious Arab
attack on the Israeli athletes at Munich's Olympic Village,
the equally disastrous attack on a passenger plane by the
Israelis — all suggest that we live in a world that sees too
many international situations quickly escalating out of control.
For an interesting elaboration of this theme, try
George MacBeth's Sf poem "Crabapple Crisis," in which
war is reduced to the micro-cosmic level of a neighborhood squabble over crabapples. The altercation over the
apples progressively escalates to the point of total annihilation. The poem's theme is very similar to that of Norman
McLaren's film, Neighbors, in which war erupts over — of
all things — a flower. Like the people in "Crab-Apple
Crisis," the film's neighbors destroy each other's property,
families — and one another. "So it goes." What is particularly useful about MacBeth's poem is that he draws obvious
parallels between the neighborhood altercation and the international scene.

Student Response:

Ask students to analyze how an international incident
might get out of hand. What role does the mass media play
in publicizing those incidents and allowing them to become
critical? It took days for the American people to hear about
the sinking of the Maine in Havana Harbor, but it takes only
hours — sometimes only minutes — for the impact of major
events to reach us today. This speed in reporting events
has its consequences in creating an immediate level of
extreme tension.

Technology, too, Leads to Destruction

Our very love of technology, which has been discussed in other chapters of this book, also could be a culprit in leading us down the wayward path to destruction. Man's technological genius seems to have been best applied to developing weapons, so that we seem to have an emotional dependence upon them. Even some post offices have defused missiles erected in front as monuments — but monuments to <u>what</u>?

In Norman Spinard's "The Big Flash," the theme of learning to like the bomb — nay, <u>love</u> the bomb — is brilliantly developed. In this story, not only do people learn to love the bomb, but they want to embrace it with fervent passion. What is unique about the story is that a rock group called "The Four Horsemen" becomes an overnight T.V. sensation by singing songs about "The Bomb." The group sweeps viewers along in an emotional orgy to the ultimate point of BANG!

Don't forget, either, that <u>Dr. Strangelove</u> develops much the same theme; the rest of the title of the book and film is: <u>How I Learned to Stop Worrying and Love the Bomb.</u> Absurd? Think about the implications of this truth: every new war machine, from the gun and tank to the airplane and atomic bomb, has actually been used.

There are other Sf stories about the ultimate weapons which are not atomic weapons. In E. B. White's "The Supremacy of Uruguay," a man discovers that noise can be a powerful weapon. So planes fly overhead, blaring out sheer waves of noise which deafen and defeat the country's enemies, until Uruguay becomes one of the world's strongest nations. Kurt Vonnegut, in "Report on the Barnhouse Effect," tells the story of a professor who discovers dynamopsychism — the ability, through the force of mind, to actually knock bombers out of the sky. In effect, the professor himself becomes a new weapon, and sets nations clamoring for his secret.

Student Response:

Ask your students for reasons why nations are so dependent on weapons. What does this dependency bode for the future? What should be done with men like Professor Barnhouse, who invent new "ultimate" weapons? Should we honor them with medals? Should they be censured? Should we try to find a way of controlling technology so that new weapons are not invented? How do your students feel about the United States' engaging in biological research with lethal viruses, such as bubonic plague, for use as potential weapons? How about the testing — or use — of nerve gas and defoliants? Do students remember the incident in Colorado in which sheep were killed by nerve gas? What should be done with these weapons?

Mistrust Brings About Nuclear Disaster

A third way in which a nuclear disaster might come about is through a malignant mistrust that seems to permeate modern technological societies. Everything from industrial spying to the billions of dollars we spend each year on defense must be subsumed under the rubric <u>mistrust</u>. While Walter Van Tillburg Clark's "The Portable Phonograph" is not ostensibly about nuclear destruction, it is about lack of trust. Some kind of war has destroyed civilization, but the survivors still remember with special sadness how things were. One of the men in the story keeps some books and a portable phonograph in his cave and three friends visit him to listen to the weekly ritual playing of one of a dozen old records. While the phonograph is important to the men because it keeps them from forgetting, it also makes the owner vulnerable. At the end of the story the phonograph's owner replaces it in a special niche in his cave and turns in for the night, and only then do we find that he has a weapon hidden for protection from his fellows. Why might his friends want the phonograph? Would they be willing to kill for it? What are men in our world willing to kill for? Why?

Student Response:

In the eventuality of a serious disaster, what five things — and five things only — would your students take with them? Why? If students begin talking about weapons, follow up with an examination of the reasons why. What does this decision say about their degree of trust? We don't need to read John Locke or Thomas Hobbes to address ourselves to the question of man's goodness. We remember an interview with a fall-out shelter owner who had a small arsenal cached away in his shelter. When asked why, he indicated that he expected to need protection from his neighbors in case of a nuclear attack. While we are not suggesting that this attitude is a popular one, it does bear examination in the classroom.

Even on the everyday level, we can't absolve ourselves and say: "Certainly I am not guilty of that kind of mistrust." While there were many acts of kindness during a major blizzard in the Chicago area a few years ago, at the same time hordes of consumers descended upon the grocery stores and almost literally stripped them of food. Does this event suggest what would happen in a case of general disaster? Every man for himself? If you have seen the film <u>Panic in the Year Zero</u>, with Ray Milland, you remember that Milland was turned from a law-abiding citizen to a man willing to commit murder for the sake of his family, all as the result of a nuclear disaster.

What of trust on the international scene? Eric Fromm contends that nations can go collectively mad. He suggests that one aspect of the Cold War has been a kind of paranoia that has affected both the Soviet Union and the United States. We certainly can see this madness in the arms race: one nation builds ballistic missiles, the other anti-ballistic missiles; the first, anti-anti-ballistic missiles, and the other now must build anti-anti-anti-ballistic missiles.

78

Discrimination — A Form of Mistrust

In most works of Sf, whenever extra-terrestrial beings are encountered by humans, the other worlders almost always are hostile. Interestingly, too, they almost always are depicted as physically deviant from the earthly "norm," and frequently are portrayed as having super-human intelligence or strength. George Kennan, the diplomat, has suggested that this is the same kind of attitude most Americans adopted toward the enemy in World War II and the Cold War; that is, an idea was created in the minds of the people that the enemy was super-evil and super-powerful and, therefore, whatever means we used to vanquish him were justifiable. Shades of Vietnam, where it was argued that killing babies was permissible because the enemy was everywhere.

Student Response:

Films such as It Came from Outer Space can be used effectively to mine the theme of discrimination against people who are physically deviant. In this movie, alien beings — again looking very strange indeed — are trying to escape from Earth, but are afraid to show themselves to Earthmen for fear of being killed.

Finally, to lend some factual evidence to this chapter, ask students to look at Robert Jay Lifton's Death in Life (Vintage). Lifton, a psychiatrist, spent considerable time in Japan interviewing the victims of World War II's atom bombings. He brilliantly examines the experiences of these people, including a group called the "living dead" — that group of people who were actually in Hiroshima or who entered it soon after the atom bomb was detonated. Almost 30 years later, these people still are very much discriminated against. Of course, John Hersey's Hiroshima (Bantam) is recognized as a classic which every student should read. Also highly recommended are Hiroshima: A Study in Science, Politics and the Ethics of War by Jonathan Harris (Addison-Wesley); Hiroshima Diary by Michihiko Hachiya (University of North Carolina Press); and We of Nagasaki by Taskashi Magai (Hawthorn). We also want to recommend Kuroi Ame's Black Rain (Kodansha International, Tokyo), a fine Japanese novel about the atomic bombing of Hiroshima.

Bibliography

Boulle, Pierre, Planet of the Apes, Signet.

Bradbury, Ray, "The Highway," The Illustrated Man, Bantam; also in Above the Human Landscape: A Social Science Fiction Anthology, Willis McNelly and Leon Stover (eds.), Goodyear.

——, "There Will Come Soft Rains," The Martian Chronicles, Bantam.

Brown, Frederic, untitled story in Science Fiction: What It's All About, Sam J. Lundwall, Ace, p. 13.

Disch, Thomas, "The Number You Have Reached," Fun with Your New Head, Signet; also in World's Best Science Fiction: Fourth Edition, Donald Wollheim and Terry Carr (eds.), Ace.

Leiber, Fritz, "A Bad Day for Sales," Nightmare Age, Frederik Pohl, Ballantine; also in 50 Short Science Fiction Tales, Isaac Asimov and Groff Conklin (eds.), Collier.

MacBeth, George, "Crab-Apple Crisis, Science Fiction: The Future, Dick Allen (ed.), Harcourt-Brace.

Merril, Judith, "That Only a Mother," Science Fiction Hall of Fame, Robert Silverberg (ed.), Avon.

Miller, Walter, A Canticle for Leibowitz, Bantam.

Roshwald, Mordecai, Level Seven, Signet.

Shute, Neville, On the Beach, Bantam.

Spinard, Norman, "The Big Flash," Voyages: Scenarios for a Ship Called Earth, Rob Sauer (ed.), Ballantine; also in Orbit 5, Damon Knight (ed.), Berkley; and World's Best Science Fiction, Donald Wollheim and Terry Carr (eds.), Ace.

Van Tillburg Clark, Walter, "The Portable Phonograph," Timeless Stories for Today and Tomorrow, Ray Bradbury (ed.), Bantam.

Vonnegut, Kurt, "Report on the Barnhouse Effect," Welcome to the Monkey House, Dell.

White, E. B., "Supremacy of Uruguay," Eco-Fiction, John Stadler (ed.), Washington Square Press; also in Timeless Stories for Today and Tomorrow, Ray Bradbury (ed.), Bantam.

Chapter 7

SQUARE PEGS AND ROUND HOLES: SOCIAL ORDER AND CONTROL
Learning How to "Fit in" to Society

Every society faces the delicate dilemma of allowing enough individual freedom to its members so that they can express and fulfill themselves, and at the same time preventing society itself from collapsing into the law of the jungle. This chapter examines how the Sf writer has dealt with the topics of social order and control and, conversely, deviance and nonconformity. Just how do a society's members learn how to fit in? What is right and what is wrong? What is acceptable and what is not acceptable? What is normal behavior and what is not normal?

Every society has its outcasts and pariahs who are rejected — sometimes far more promptly than they are in our own — because of their deviance. Among the Bambuti of the Ituri forest, for example, a person who is essentially independent is rejected from the society. Colin Turnbull, in his book The Forest People, mentions a hunter who is so expert that he can kill more game than anybody else. When the man breaks away from the group hunt to make additional kills, he is immediately ostracized. Why? Because the Bambuti realize that if each man were to follow his personal whims, the nexus holding the group together would dissolve and the group itself would perish.

How do children learn to fit into their society? Harvard's Lawrence Kohlberg has concerned himself with this question. While he has done much of his work with American children, he also has conducted cross-cultural studies in Mexico and Taiwan. We use Kohlberg's series of stages of moral development to analyze this chapter's Sf stories; at what stage of moral development, we have asked, do the characters in a particular Sf story seem to be?

Six Stages of Moral Development:

The first stage of Kohlberg's scheme is punishment. A child learns quickly that when he does wrong he is punished, either physically or verbally. Unfortunately, it appears that too many adults never grow out of this stage. They remain adults who believe that punishment is the only way to make anybody behave; the battered child syndrome is the sick extension of this attitude. But how many of us still think that the only way to make a child or adult behave is through punishment? As a child grows older, he also learns that when he does right he is rewarded, and when he does wrong rewards may be withheld. This is stage two. To some, rewards become all important. If a child behaves, he is given things; if he misbehaves, things — sometimes even love — are withheld. These first two stages are listed by Kohlberg under the rubric "Pre-Conventional."

Kohlberg calls his next two stages "Conventional" because most people operate in this area most of the time. Stage three is the "nice boy, nice girl" stage, in which children are taught the tenets of proper behavior. "Nice little boys don't do this." "Nice little girls don't do that." This attitude can, of course, be carried to an absurd point, too: Willy Loman, in Death of a Salesman, thinks that the only important thing in life is to be well-liked. How often have we expressed approval of someone simply by saying that he or she is "nice"? What does the word mean? Stage four is the "law and order" stage, in which the child becomes aware that there are certain rules and regulations which each person must obey. It is at this stage that the child becomes aware that there exist authority figures, in the guise of teachers and policemen, who enforce the rules. Often, however, people cling so tenaciously to this stage that the letter of the law kills its spirit. A few short years ago, for example, many high schools were embroiled in the great hair issue; the question of whether or not students could wear their hair as long as they wanted. To many critics, the issue was simply that because schools had regulations against long hair, that was all there was to it; the proponents of long hair, however, seemed to be arguing that we must change the rules to reflect the times.

The last two stages of development — the "Post-Conventional," as Kohlberg calls them — are perhaps the most interesting. They call for a certain sophisticated subtlety which most people are incapable of achieving until their twenties, if at all; for that reason, these stages are relatively unconventional. Stage five is the "social contract" stage, in which a man obeys because he understands that if nobody obeyed any rule or law, we would quickly deteriorate into the chaos of anomie, or normlessness. This recognition is much more subtle than stage four, in which we obey simply because a law is a law. Finally, in stage six, we reach the rarified plains of universal principles, where one begins to appreciate that there are certain principles which contribute to the uniqueness of man. It is asserted at this stage, for example, that there are certain acts humans should not inflict on one another simply because we share an essential humanity. For further details on Kohlberg's studies, see his article in Psychology Today (September, 1968), or the recent pamphlet "Moral Reasoning," published by AEP (Xerox).

What Is Crime?

Perhaps the obvious place to start an examination of order and control is with the criminal; for that reason we pose the question: what is a crime in the Sf world, and how are criminal types treated by their society? Remember, though, that what we are really after is some kind of commentary on American society and our understanding of the concepts of crime and criminality.

In Ron Goulart's "Into the Shop," automatic police cars apprehend, try, convict and, yes, even execute criminals in the back seat — then neatly spit out the ashes in little urns. Unfortunately, one such car goes berserk and begins executing the wrong people. This story is an incisive commentary not only on man and the machine, but also on one common view of criminal justice — that it should be swift and lethal.

Another interesting aspect of capital punishment is found in Larry Niven's "The Jigsaw Man." In this story, organ transplants have become so commonplace that human sources for the organs have become scarce. As a result,

84

criminals literally are dissected for their organs, and these are stored away in organ banks. "Organlegging," a take-off on "bootlegging," becomes popular, and people are waylaid on the streets and carved up for spare parts. The society in the story finally reaches the absurd point where capital punishment is meted out for running red lights and speeding — just so that additional organs will be available for those who want them.

Student Response:

Historically, for what crimes was capital punishment used? In our society, for what crimes do you think it should be used? Why? How should criminals be treated? What is your definition of a crime? An overwhelming number of crimes in this country are "white-collar" crimes: embezzling, cheating on one's income tax, padding one's expense account, bribery, etc. Are these crimes as serious as armed robbery? Would you treat "white-collar" criminals as harshly as other criminals? How should corporate crimes, such as price fixing, be handled? Sociologists talk about "crimes without victims", drug addiction, prostitution, alcoholism, consenting homosexuality. What, if anything, should be done with people who commit these "crimes"? Should they be put in jail? Which crimes do you find most distasteful? Least objectionable? Which crimes could you tolerate? Using Kohlberg's stages of moral development, explain why so many aspects of our penal system are devoted to punishment.

The Effects of Technology on Crime

Joe Valachi, in The Valachi Papers, mentions that in the 1920s criminals could just ride up to a fur store, break the window, and steal the furs. At this time, criminals possessed fast cars and many policemen were still on bicycles. When the police began using radios to apprehend criminals, the criminals began using radios to monitor the police calls. Elaborate burglar alarm systems were installed by businesses, and burglars perfected new techniques for circumventing them. So it goes in a technological society. As we saw in "Gadget vs. Trend" (cited in Chapter 4), we can't always predict the effect of a technological change on all segments of the society.

Student Response:

What crimes do your students see becoming more important in the future? How might the computer both thwart and encourage crime? How about Dick Tracy-kinds of inventions, such as wrist radios? What will they be like? Might Goulart's automatic police cars actually be invented?

In Lloyd Biggle's story, "The Perfect Punishment," a man accused of murder is sent for punishment to another planet, where each criminal is assigned a quota of crimes he must commit. If one is guilty of robbery, he must commit a quota of robberies each week. Humans, also known as Type Bs, may commit crimes only against Type As, which we later discover are really androids. (The Type Bs, however, never make this discovery.) In the story, a convicted murderer — who has lost his plea of innocence — wrestles long and hard with his conscience over his quota of murders. The more he procrastinates, the higher his quota becomes, until finally he simply refuses to kill. Only then do we find that this action is the litmus test: when an offender refuses to commit a crime, it is assumed that he is cured. Unfortunately, once the man is told of his cure, he goes berserk and begins killing androids with great relish.

Student Response:

What do your students think of this sort of punishment? Ask them to list the attitude toward criminals a person on each of Kohlberg's levels would have. What, for example, would be the attitude of a person on stage two? Five? Six?

Crime Novels Featuring Futuristic Twists:

Two crime novels which should be mentioned here are Alfred Bester's The Demolished Man and Hal Clement's Needle. In Bester's book, the police have the ability to read minds; as a result, crime is unknown — until one Raskolnikov-type decides to commit the perfect crime. In Needle, a criminal virus comes to Earth and hides in a human body, while a detective virus in hot pursuit does the same. Looking for a wayward virus is like looking for the proverbial needle; hence the title of the book.

Isaac Asimov also has contributed two crime novels to this genre: The Caves of Steel and its sequel, The Naked Sun. Caves of Steel features an android detective who matches wits with a human counterpart in trying to solve a very touchy murder case. In The Naked Sun, the same two protagonists are paired to solve a crime on another planet.

In Donald Westlake's "The Winner," a unique form of control is used for those considered to be politically persona non grata. A black box is placed in the political criminal's body; when he strays too far from his assigned territory, terrible wracking pains shoot through his body, driving him back to "home" ground. No need for conventional-type prisons in Westlake's world.

Student Response:

Besides prisons, what other forms of treatment for criminal behavior can your students think of? What about Westlake's idea? Ask them to list its good and bad points. What might go wrong with an idea like this? Think of all the possibilities you can.

Categorizing Nonconformity

But how does society view other kinds of deviant behavior, short of criminality? Perhaps the Sf writer offers us even more challenging ideas here. What of the nonconformist? What of the maverick and rebel? Sociologist Robert Merton has devised an interesting scheme which works well here. He places people into five categories; the first category is the conformist, who agrees with the goals of the society and also with the means used to achieve those goals. Merton's second category is that of the innovator, who agrees with the goals of society but, for one reason or another, is denied the means to achieve those goals — so he innovates, and finds new means to reach the goals. A good example of this category is the Mafia. Some members of this secret society live in suburbia, drive big cars, own beautiful houses, send their children to private schools; the only difference is that they reached these goals in an unconventional way. The immigrant Irish achieved the same goals through the political machine.

The third category is that of the ritualist, who has lost sight of the goals and is hung up on the means. The man wedded to the Protestant ethic, for example — who insists upon hard work for the sake of hard work — may well have lost sight of why he is working so hard. Fourth, then, is the retreatist, who says, "I disagree with both the goals and the means of the society" — and "drops out." These people are few indeed — Henry David Thoreau was one, as were some of the Bohemians of the 1920s; perhaps some of today's "hippies" also qualify. Merton's last group is the reformer, who says, "I, too, disagree with the goals and means of the society, but I am going to set up new goals and new means to reach those goals." Perhaps the Yippies, of recent political fame, fit this category.

Student Response:

As students read Sf stories for this section, ask them to consider not only Kohlberg's stages of moral development, but also Merton's system of categories.

Dealing with Deviance

In Damon Knight's "Country of the Kind," "deviant" types are forced to give off such a powerful stench that "normal" people withdraw in horror and repulsion. This is comparable to Lombroso's discredited attempt to relate criminal behavior to body type by stating that people who are criminal in thought or action also look like criminals. In Knight's story, people who are deviant smell like deviants.

In "To See the Invisible Man," Robert Silverberg portrays a man stigmatized by his society because of his lack of human warmth. He is punished by having a symbol branded on his forehead; thus he is made "invisible" for one year. Although the man is physically visible, nobody may have any contact with him; he may wander into a restaurant kitchen to eat right out of the pot, but he may not go out front and expect to be seated by the management. Even when he falls ill, no doctor may care for him.

Harlan Ellison offers his method of future social control in the excellently written "'Repent, Harlequin,' Said the Ticktockman." One man refuses to be slotted into his proper place in a highly mechanistic world which places such a high premium on punctuality that people who can't be on time have all the minutes and hours they are late tallied up; at a certain lethal point, their "cardio-plates" are inserted into the great computer and they are shut off. POW! The mischievous harlequin delights in antics which gum up the works. One of his favorite frolics, for example, is dropping jelly beans onto the city's moving sidewalks and slowing everything down by seven minutes. Finally, he, too, is shut off. At the story's end, we are left with a subtle suspicion that the chief timekeeper, the ticktockman, really is a robot: when his secretary informs him that he is behind time in his appointments, his only reply is "Mrmee, Mree." Perhaps it's the hum of a motor? Or could he be just a human who's spent too much time with machines?

Student Response:

What are some of the subtle ways we learn about control? Why do we place so much stress on punctuality? When is it all right to be late? To what places might one be permitted to arrive late? How late is late?

"Harrison Bergeron," one of Kurt Vonnegut's heroes, is too intelligent and too handsome in a society where everybody is supposed to be equal. As with all intelligent and handsome people in this society, Bergeron is penalized with thick glasses, heavy weights hanging from his body, and a grotesque mask. Other people who act in too nonconformist a manner have their brains blasted by an assorted cacaphony of noises, ringing bells, and erupting cannons. On a nationwide T.V. show, Bergeron breaks free of his shackles and, after briefly soaring in dance with a beautiful ballerina, he is killed by the Handicapper General.

"Profession," by Isaac Asimov, proposes an "Education Day," on which all 18-year-olds are programmed for their life's profession. With nail-biting anticipation, the young men file into a room where they are tested to find out what they are going to be. Each year, however, a few students are discovered who don't have the right brain-wave patterns to be anything; these "unfortunates" are placed in their own sanctuary to read and think. However pleasing that might be to us, to them it is the worst stigma of all.

Student Response:

Ask your students how people are slotted into their proper places in the United States? Often, when we attend parties, the first question asked of us is, "What do you do?" Why do others want to know this? Can anybody be <u>anything</u> he or she wants? Are too-intelligent people penalized in this society? What do you think of the idea behind Asimov's "Education Day"? Might it not save a lot of time, energy, and money? (Incidentally, a machine now has been developed, and is being used in Latin America and some American cities, to predict with some accuracy who has the intelligence to do what — or so its inventor claims. It is not an I.Q. test, but an actual machine which samples the efficiency of brain waves through electrodes attached to the subject's head.)

Classic Novels of Static Society

If your students have not read some of the classic Sf novels dealing with order and control, this is a good place to recommend that they do so. Obviously, Aldous Huxley's <u>Brave New World</u> must be included here. God is dead in Huxley's world; He has been replaced by "Great Ford," the symbol of pernicious capitalism, mass production, and conformity. Malcontents are put away on reservations, and embryos are grown artificially so that people can be genetically designed to fit society's needs. If a batch of rocket engineers is wanted, the government merely has the hatchery decant them. Lest children become unhappy with their class or job, they are raised in dormitories where they can be conditioned not only to accept their status, but to love it. In the truest sense of the term, this is a static society — all flows smoothly and there is no room for change. Order rules supreme.

In this book, the drug "soma" is used to keep people under control and "happy." The drug makes them content with their lives and turns them into intellectual vegetables who don't question, don't fear, don't rebel — just exist. Since <u>Brave New World</u>, many Sf stories have been written using the drug theme as a form of control. Perhaps one of the best of these is Frederik Pohl's "What To Do Until the Analyst Comes." In this story, "Cheery Gum" is invented, a non-addictive drug which makes all people happy by keeping them on a perpetual high. Everyone is so high and so happy that psychiatrists are unemployed, planes fall from the sky, and cars run off the roads. Everybody is just too happy. Absurd? Just a few years ago, Omaha and other U.S. cities were experimenting on their school children with behavior control drugs to "shape-up" the "problem" kids; many adults swallow tranquilizers (soma?) in great quantities. We have drugs to put us to sleep and drugs to wake us up; drugs for headaches and drugs for nervous tension — drugs to keep us up and drugs to keep us down.

George Orwell's 1984 introduces another static society, in which "Big Brother" employs electronic devices to spy on people. There is no escape from his all-seeing eye, and there is no such thing as privacy. People have been conditioned out of anything as silly as love; except for love of the state and of "Big Brother," all human emotions have become suspect. If one insists on being recalcitrant he is swiftly dealt with. Winston Smith, one such misfit, falls in love with a woman and, consequently, calls the system's premises into question. Through fear he, too, is brainwashed into "loving" his "Big Brother." Smith has a terrible phobia about rats, so rats it is for Smith; finally, he collapses when he is threatened with the rats, and admits the "goodness" of "Big Brother" and the state. Only then can he be put to death as a heretic, for he has admitted his evil ways and recanted.

Other Classics Which Supplement Science Fiction

We suggest that two other classics be used in this unit to amplify the ideas found in Sf works. The first is Plato's Apology, in which Socrates refuses to confess his "guilt" in corrupting Athens' youth, so he is sentenced to swallow the lethal hemlock for his "crimes."

Student Response:

Should Socrates have been put to death? Why? What crimes did he commit? What should the role of "gadfly" be in any society? Do you know anyone who is a gadfly? How is he treated by today's society?

The second recommended classic is Bertolt Brecht's play, "Galileo." Galileo brings the Catholic church's whole position on cosmology into question when he proves the heliocentric theory of the universe, as opposed to the geocentric theory upheld by the Church.

When faced with the Inquisition, Galileo renounces his theory but, sotto voce, he says that he is still right. While Socrates has died a martyr's death, Galileo lives on to perpetuate his theories and raise people's doubts, even if only surreptitiously. Robert Bolt's "A Man for All Seasons" also could be used here; Thomas More's struggle against the state is comparable to Galileo's problem with the church.

Student Response:

Ask students who took the "better" position, Galileo or Socrates? In their opinion, what should be done with men whose ideas oppose those of their static society? Should they be imprisoned? Executed? Banished? Should they be subjected to Donald Westlake's treatment? Set free? Honored? Ask students to consider some more immediate examples of man in conflict with the state: what of Daniel Ellsberg, the Berrigan brothers, and others like them? Can we allow men such as these to divulge "secret" information about the state? What does the word "subversive" mean? How should we control "subversive" ideas? "Subversive" men? Or should we control them at all? To some people, Ralph Nader is "subversive" because he questions many of the very basic premises of our economic and political systems. What do you think about people like Nader?

A la 1984, should we use electronic devices for spying on "suspect" people? Think back to the uproar of recent years, when the army admitted spying upon civilians, and the Republicans upon the Democrats at the Watergate. Is this action right? Why? Recently we heard that the U. S. government was considering placing an electronic device in every home, car, boat, and plane so that the public could be warned immediately of a national emergency. While spokesmen for the administration disclaimed any intention of carrying out this project, they did admit that a report outlining the idea had been submitted for study. What do your students think of this idea? What might be some of its drawbacks? Some people feel that this idea would be just one more electronic nudge toward 1984; what do your students think?

A View of Subversion of the Future

You also might consider reading Bradbury's classic Fahrenheit 451, in which firemen rush out, not to save lives, but to burn books. Here, books are subversive. Once people begin reading books, they rub their minds against new ideas, and in a static society new ideas are anathema. Consequently, some rebels retreat into the woods to memorize books verbatim; to join this deviant subsociety, one also must memorize a book.

Student Response:

Can ideas be "subversive"? What about books? Are there any books your students would consider banning? Which ones? Why? Should pornographic books be banned? Are they harmful to people? If students were to live in Bradbury's subgroup, what book would each pick to memorize for posterity? Why?

Censoring Violence

While many liberals are almost genetically opposed to censoring political or sexual materials, they are not so willing to allow violent films and books to remain unchecked. With the recent spate of political murders, many people argue that the media, in particular — from Westerns showing the slaughtering of Indians, to gore-drenched childrens' cartoon shows — have conditioned us to tolerate still more violence. Consequently, they argue, we must begin censoring gross acts of mayhem and murder, particularly those shown on T.V. Ask your students to look through newspaper movie ads and note the number of violent acts depicted there. On a recent Friday we counted seven pistols, nine shotguns and rifles blazing, one man being bombed by three helicopters, one man being kicked in the face, and assorted other violent acts and instruments in the movie ads. Replacing the Western "good guys," once pictured gunning down "bad guys" in the ads, is a new trend toward showing ghoulish monsters, fangs dripping blood, ripping out girls' necks, decapitating people, running them through buzz saws, etc.

Student Response:

Should violent T.V. programs be censored? What about movies? Should make-believe murders be shown on T.V.? How about the actual murders sometimes captured by T.V. news cameras? Should these pictures be shown? How about those taken at gory accident scenes? After Jayne Mansfield was decapitated, one Chicago newspaper ran a picture on page 1 showing Miss Mansfield's head on her car's hood. Should that photo have been allowed to be printed?

Dealing with Computer Technology

One last potential instrument of social order and control is the electronic computer. To what extent should computers be used to store up massive amounts of information about one's credit, political beliefs, and personal habits? While the data bank behemoths have been dealt with in Chapter 4, this one aspect of "Man or the Machine?" is included here.

In his Sf story "Franchise," Isaac Asimov tells of a society where people don't have to vote any more. Through the use of electronic projections, computers have become so sophisticated that voters just aren't necessary. Multivac can do it all. Just one voter is needed for the machine to "correct" for the human factor, so every four years a "Voter of the Year" is selected. A week before the elections, his house is cordoned off and he is prevented from receiving any news for the rest of the week. On election day, he is taken to an installation to confront Multivac, which asks him a series of questions, many of which may seem absurd — and from this interview, all of the elections, local, state, and national, are decided. Of course, the "Voter of the Year" receives all kinds of publicity and money, but he also suffers all the slings and arrows of an outraged public if the politicians he helps to elect turn out badly.

The Man Who Never Rocked the Boat

We often end this particular unit with a consideration of W. H. Auden's poem, "The Unknown Citizen." The state erects a monument to him because he never rocked the boat and has always held the proper views. This is the man who never could be charged with an unconventional thought. Auden concludes with: "Was he free? Was he happy? The question is absurd: Had anything been wrong, we should certainly have heard."

Student Response:

Ralph Waldo Emerson once said that the way to judge a society was not by its census or by its monuments (nor, we might add, by its GNP), but by the quality of the man it produces. Using both Emerson's statement and Auden's poem, ask your students as a culminating activity to consider just what kind of man or woman is being produced in the United States today. Which values are stressed? Which are ignored? What kinds of values get the rewards? Would you mind living next door to W. H. Auden's "unknown citizen"? Would you marry him or her? After all, following Merton's scheme of categorizing nonconformity, he or she is the very personification of the conformist and good citizen.

Bibliography

Asimov, Isaac, The Caves of Steel, Fawcett.
_____, "Franchise," The Sociology of the Possible, Richard Ofshe (ed.), Harcourt-Brace.
_____, The Naked Sun, Fawcett.
_____, "Profession," The Sociology of the Possible, Richard Ofshe (ed.), Harcourt-Brace.
Bester, Alfred, The Demolished Man, Signet.
Biggle, Lloyd, "The Perfect Punishment," The Rule of the Door and Other Fanciful Regulations, Doubleday.
Bradbury, Ray, Fahrenheit 451, Ballantine.
Clement, Hal, The Needle, Lancer.
Ellison, Harlan, "'Repent, Harlequin,' Said the Ticktock-man," World's Best Science Fiction: Second Series, Donald Wollheim and Terry Carr (eds.), Ace; also in Science Fiction: The Future, Dick Allen (ed.), Harcourt-Brace.

Goulart, Ron, "Into the Shop," Broke Down Engine and
Other Troubles with Machines, Colliers; also in Spectrum
Four, Kingsley Amis and Robert Conquest (eds.), Berkley.

Huxley, Aldous, Brave New World, Bantam.

Knight, Damon, "The Country of the Kind," Science Fiction
Hall of Fame, Robert Silverberg (ed.), Avon.

Orwell, George, 1984, NAL.

Pohl, Frederik, "What to Do Until the Analyst Comes,"
17X Infinity, Groff Conklin (ed.), Dell; also in The Sociology of the Possible, Richard Ofshe (ed.), Prentice-Hall.

Silverberg, Robert, "To See the Invisible Man," SF: Authors'
Choice 2, Harry Harrison (ed.), Berkley.

Vonnegut, Kurt, "Harrison Bergeron," Welcome to the
Monkey House, Dell; also in Science Fiction: The Future,
Dick Allen (ed.), Harcourt-Brace.

Westlake, Donald, "The Winner," Nova I: An Anthology of
Original SF Stories, Harry Harrison (ed.), Delacorte.

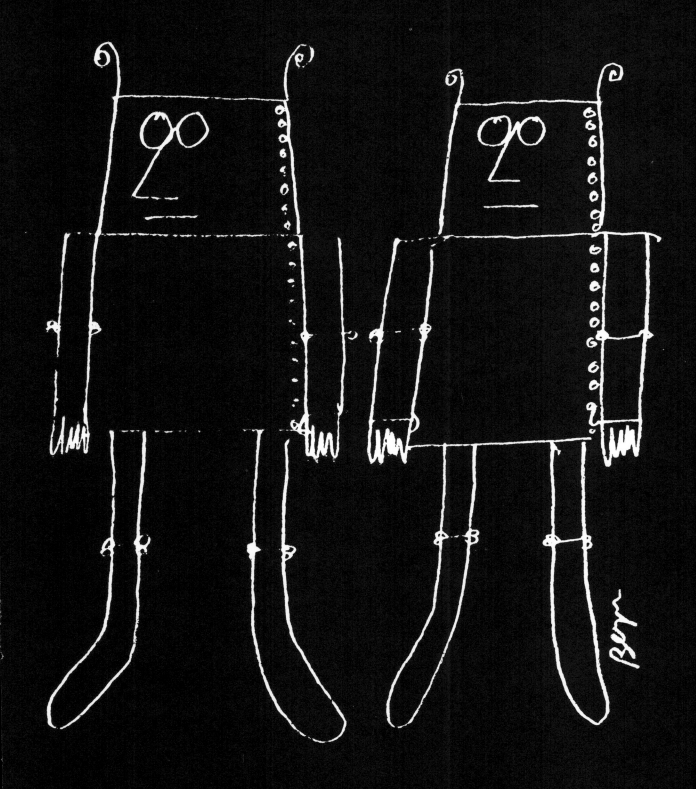

Chapter 8

ALL ROBOTS LOOK ALIKE: PREJUDICE
Generating Tolerance and Compassion...

Perhaps one of the most desirable goals teachers attempt to achieve is to make their students more tolerant of one another. Of course, we have seen much stress in recent years regarding racial tolerance, but we all recognize that there are other kinds of tolerance which we should seek: tolerance of one social class for another, tolerance of different political philosophies, even tolerance these days of one sex for the other. Unfortunately, when we try teaching about prejudice, we immediately find ourselves embroiled in deep emotions, passions, and hatreds. Further complications arise because the immense amount of available information most of us have been subjected to has contributed to student apathy toward this topic. Through Sf, one often can approach the topic of prejudice and, implicitly, compassion, without the blinders springing up so fast. After all, when you are discussing prejudice toward robots or invisible men, nobody feels very threatened, so explosive situations are temporarily set aside.

... Through an Understanding of Genetic Conditioning

One of the most successful books we have used in developing this theme is Brave New World. We don't use the entire novel with this chapter, only that part which describes the genetic conditioning of the society's members. As we indicated in Chapter 7, embryos are grown artificially in Huxley's world, and his society is divided into five classes: Alphas, Betas, Gammas, Deltas, and Epsilons.

Alphas do the most intellectual jobs; Epsilons do the menial and dirty work. Children are further conditioned in the state nurseries through Pavlovian reinforcement of their place in life. Delta babies, for example, are placed on the floor amidst books and flowers, which Deltas aren't supposed to like. When the tots crawl toward these tantalizing objects and touch them, alarm bells clang and mild electric shocks are administered, sending the babies into paroxysms of terror. While older children are sleeping, they get their dose of reinforcement too: "elementary class consciousness" is droned into their unconscious heads. Each of the classes wears a uniform of a different color, and class prejudice is continuously stressed: Betas are informed during "class consciousness" that Alphas are better and work harder, and that Gammas, Deltas, and Epsilons are inferior. Other classes also are appropriately conditioned toward each other.

Student Response:

Ask your students: What is your honest opinion of Huxley's society? What would you want to be in Huxley's world: an Alpha, Beta, Gamma, Delta, or Epsilon? Why? Ask students to assign occupations from our society to Huxley's classes. (Generally, students categorize physicians and lawyers as Alphas; technicians with high skills are Betas; managers, salesmen, and office workers become Deltas; skilled laborers are Gammas; and unskilled workers are relegated to the Epsilon class.) Occasionally, of course, a teacher gets a maverick class that wants to assign Alpha status to artists and poets. In Huxley's world, though, there were no poets or artists because they were viewed as a threat to the static society. To further involve students with the concept of genetic engineering, we have designed and used a simulation game (see Appendix 3) which complements Huxley's book.

Discovering Status Differences in America's Caste System

Along with Huxley's book we use articles about the Indian caste system; but with both Brave New World and the caste system, we deliberately shy away from racial topics. We want students to react first to the unfamiliar caste systems before a connection is made with the American class/caste system, which is based on race and education. In this way we believe that students react less emotionally to our own caste problems and are more willing to engage in calm deliberation. The individual teacher will want to make his own transition to the real problems of race relations in contemporary America; we often use materials like Ralph Ellison's The Invisible Man, or read sections of Richard Wright's Native Son to students. In particular, we use the section of Wright's novel in which Bigger and his friend Gus discuss a skywriting plane and automatically assume the pilot is white. After all, they reason, the whites have all the good jobs. Teachers also might try using some selections from The Autobiography of Malcolm X. The section in which the author describes his experiences when he was living with a white family as a youth is most relevant. At this point in his life, Malcolm X was thought of as a good "nigger" who knew his place. We also use newspaper articles which show the inequality between black and white schools, and the income differences between races. Teachers should be able to find similar examples for their own local area.

Student Response:

Some key questions for this section are: What is your definition of status? Is there an American caste system? Describe it. Who belongs where in it? Ask students to try to write an Sf story on the American caste system. For ideas on how to begin, they might read "The Midas Plague" (cited in Chapter 9). Ask students how does one win or lose status in American society? Why do sports stars have such high status in America and elsewhere in today's world? Sociologists talk about status inconsistency, a state in which a man may make a lot of money but not receive political and economic status commensurate with his salary. Can you think of any people or occupations in America which show status inconsistency?

One additional way to approach status is through a role-playing activity we sometimes use. Ask students to role-play their 10th high school reunion. What immediately comes out here is that all-important question: "What do you do?" If one were to answer, "I love, I enjoy the sun, I partake of this good green Earth," he would be thought of as a bit tipsy or weird. What actually is meant by the question is, "What job do you hold?" Knowing another person's job is a handy form of shorthand which allows us to slot people in their "proper" places.

Different Aspects of Prejudice

There are many fine Sf novels and short stories which deal with different facets of the question of prejudice. "Look, You Think You've Got Troubles," by Carol Carr, finds a Jewish Earthling's daughter running off to marry a green Martian. With hilarious complications, her mother and her resisting father take a three-month jaunt to Mars to visit the extraterrestrial couple, who are expecting their first baby. Adjustment is difficult for the father because his son-in-law is so ugly and so different; the Martian reminds the girl's father of "an acorn atop a stalk of broccoli."

Student Response:

At some point in this chapter, the teacher may wish to give students a social distance scale. This scale will measure the degree of intimacy they would allow "other" people or groups the class may be studying: blacks, whites, people of different social classes, social cliques, or even people of different ages.

One such scale is: "I would have no objection to ... (Insert the name of the group being studied)"
Strongly Agree___ Agree___ Disagree___ Strongly Disagree___

1. ... Attending class with them?
2. ... Sitting next to them in class?
3. ... Having them attend school sports events?
4. ... Walking with them?
5. ... As an individual, talking to them?
6. ... Attending a party with them?
7. ... Eating with them at the same table in the cafeteria?
8. ... Double-dating with them?
9. ... Having dates with them?
10. ... Introducing them to my relatives and/or friends?
11. ... Living next door to them?
12. ... Eventually marrying somebody from this group?

Of course, the way to indicate how effective your prejudice chapter has been is to give the social distance test again after the unit is completed.

The Effects of Prejudice on Children

In Ray Bradbury's poignant short story, "All Summer in a Day," Earth children living on Venus — a planet of almost perpetual rain — have waited almost all their lives for the sun to make an appearance, which it does for only one hour every seven years. A sensitive little girl named Margot has come to Venus years after the other children, so she remembers seeing the sun from Earth; but the other children, because they are so young, can't remember seeing it at all. Because of Margot's sensitivity and her memory of the sun, the other children dislike her. As a childish — if mean — prank, they lock her in a closet; shortly afterwards, the sun beams with all its splendor, and the children, lost in their childish frolicking, completely forget about Margot. Only when the rains begin again do they remember her, and sheepishly let her out of the dark closet.

Student Response:

Why were the children so cruel to Margot? What kinds of mean things did your students do to other children when they were small? Why? What kind of children were discriminated against when students were in elementary school? Why? How about high school? Who gets discriminated against, and why? Have students make a scale running from the most prejudiced to the least prejudiced things children do to one another. Include such things as words, taunts, and physical abuse. Most students once were told that "sticks and stones will break my bones, but names will never hurt me." Is this statement true? Countee Cullen, in his poem "Incident," tells about riding on a Baltimore streetcar as a child and smiling at a white boy, whose only response was "nigger." Ask your white students how they would have felt in Cullen's place. Ask them to think about the names they have been called or they have used about others. How have they, personally, been hurt by discrimination? Almost every child, at some point, has a story to tell about the cruel response of others to the student's physical deformities, scholastic capacities, parents' status, parents' inability to speak English, race, etc. The emotional high point of one of our classes on prejudice occurred when a nearly-blind girl voluntarily described her experiences of growing up to the taunts of "four eyes" and worse. She vividly described being bussed to a special school and set apart as a "freak," in her words.

In Isaac Asimov's "The Ugly Little Boy," an old maid nurse is hired to care for a little Neanderthal boy who has been brought into a future time for study by scientists. The little boy is so ugly that most women would shy away from him in horror, but the nurse develops a motherly love for the child. Earth children ostracize the little boy, who becomes lonely and frightened; his only contact with warmth and love is the nurse. As public outcry mounts over the boy, the scientists decide to spirit him back into time — but they know they can't replace him exactly where they found him, so their action may result in the child's death. Just as they are sending him back to his own time, the nurse jumps into the device and goes with him to care for him in a distant past she knows almost nothing about. Hers is a rare act of human love and compassion.

Student Response:

What is the most selfless act your students have performed? What is the most compassionate act they have seen one human perform for another? What were the circumstances surrounding this act?

Discrimination Against "Non-Humans"

Avram Davidson's "Now Let Us Sleep" tells of the Yahoos, semi-human creatures, who are much abused and discriminated against by Earthmen. The Yahoos live on a planet located between Earth and a prison planet, and spaceships transporting prisoners make frequent calls to the Yahoos' home so that the prisoners can exploit them. One government official, however, takes pity on the creatures and vows to save them from annihilation. After much persuasion, the government agrees to remove the Yahoos to a safe sanctuary; while the creatures are being transported to their sanctuary, however, government doctors begin innoculating the Yahoos with lethal viruses, as test cases. In an unusual act of humanity and contrition, the compassionate official decides to destroy the remaining Yahoos to spare them any more suffering. In the process, he takes his own life. Davidson says he wrote this story after hearing about the threat of extinction to aboriginal Tasmanians, but he could well have received his inspiration from the Nazi concentration camps, U. S. treatment of the American Indian, or medical experiments on syphilitic prisoners in Tuskegee, Alabama. Why did Davidson's government official commit suicide?

In Isaac Asimov's The Caves of Steel (cited in Chapter 7), a human detective named Lije Baley is forced to work with a robot named R. (for robot) Daneel Olivaw. In Asimov's society, everybody lives under domes and the "Spacers" have the upperhand. "Spacers" are the descendents of Earthmen who had journeyed into distant space years before, but who now have returned to dominate Earth. The Earth people hate the "Spacers" who live in Spacetown, an area isolated from the rest of the underground city. When an Earthman wishes to enter this forbidden province, he is literally decontaminated before he is allowed to come in. This action adds to the discomfiture of the Earth people who, naturally, don't enjoy their subservient lot in life. If the Earth folk hate "Spacers," they hate robots even more — and the "Spacers" are trying to introduce still more of the mechanical marvels into the city.

In The Caves of Steel, a "Spacer" has been murdered; this is serious business indeed because it appears, through circumstantial evidence, that an Earthman is guilty. Lije Baley is assigned to work on the case with R. Daneel. Unfortunately for Baley, the android's exceptional intelligence is exceeded only by his probing curiosity about human ways. Because R. Daneel looks so human, right down to the swirls on the palms of his hands and the tears in his eyes, nobody but Baley and his wife knows his true identity. Consequently, Baley continuously is embarrassed when he sees the robot doing things which the human detective feels should remain exclusively human. When Baley visits one of the "Personals" to shower, shave, and have his clothes freshly laundered, for example, Daneel wants to go, too; when they go to a large public eating hall, Daneel's desire to join Baley in eating food (although the robot has been programmed to remove the meal later from a special compartment) causes Baley much discomfort. His attitude is very similar to that of some whites when blacks first began integrating restaurants. As the novel develops, however, man and machine begin to appreciate the unique contribution each is making to solve the case.

Student Response:

What are Baley's special talents? R. Daneel's? How do they complement one another? In what specific ways do man and robot learn to get along? Why does Baley's wife react to R. Daneel the way she does? Do other people have any influence on our own prejudices: in other words, are there times when you would like to be friendly with "them" but are afraid of what relatives or friends might think of you? When, if ever, has this happened to you? Would it bother you to have to work with an "intelligent" robot, who might be able to work faster and more efficiently than you?

Overcoming Prejudice Through Love

Let us re-emphasize, though, that the point we are making here is not that in the near future men must learn to love robots, but that through these stories it may be easier for students to confront the more difficult questions of relations between young and old, and different races, nationalities, and social classes.

One last novel for consideration in this section is Clifford Simak's City. In this book, robots have become more intelligent than man, but dogs — that's right, dogs! — are the most intelligent life form of all, and also the most "humane," if we can apply that term to animals. These dogs are so gentle that they refuse to kill any other animals; when they teach the beasts of the forest to talk, communication leads to the abolition of killing — and carnivores become vegetarians and pacifists. Even man forgets how to kill. There are some thought-provoking incidents in the book: in one such example, a man kills a robin, thus learning about death and violence. At the conclusion of the book, the dogs face a moral dilemma of some importance: they have discovered that the ants are building a gigantic city. The dogs either must stop them or see their own civilization brought

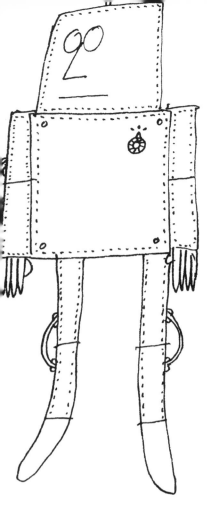

down in ruins. One old robot knows that humans once eliminated ants with poison. But should he give this answer to the dogs, who are opposed to killing? That is the question — and the dilemma to be solved.

Student Response:

Under what circumstances do prejudice and fear lead to violence? Ask students to think about Ireland, Vietnam, and Bangla Desh. Is it ever possible for radically different people to live in peace? Is it possible for men to reach the point where they won't kill? Have students write an Sf story based on the theme of no more killing.

Invisible Men and Monsters

Another interesting way of approaching prejudice is by employing the "invisible man" theme. In Richard Wilson's "See Me Not," a man awakens to find that he is invisible. After confronting his wife, he seeks medical help. Soon friend and stranger alike seek out opportunities to gape at the invisible freak. What do they expect to see? At one time, they actually catch the invisible man, beat him, and rub grass stains on him so that he can be seen.

Student Response:

Ask students what might be the reaction of the public to an invisible man? Would he be feared? Why?

At this point, the teacher might consider showing a film like It Came from Outer Space. The extraterrestrial visitors in this movie are grotesque monsters, but aren't they always when they come from "out there"? These monsters are trying to leave Earth, but they know that if they reveal their true identity to Earthmen they will be hunted down and killed. Why do we portray "other" people as the personification of evil? Why do we automatically assume that if "they" are out there, they are to be feared? What connections can your students see between this film and present-day international relations?

"It's Not Nice to Laugh ..."

The final section of this chapter can be used to introduce other cultures to students in world geography or culture courses. Additional suggestions are included to introduce an American culture course. This sub-section might well be entitled, "It's Not Nice to Laugh at Martians — or Other Folks."

Every teacher wants to make his students more sensitive to other cultures and, at the same time, hopes that students will recognize that while other cultures do things differently, they are not to be considered "funny" or "weird." Often, however, as Marshall McLuhan has told us, the medium is the message, and students allow so-called "bizarre" rituals they have seen in films and on television to get in the way of a deeper understanding of people. When the Sf medium is used first, students tend to mock less, and seem to be more willing to look at other cultures with empathy and objectivity.

We find that one of the best stories for this purpose is "Report on Grand Central Terminal," by Leo Szilard. In this story, a group of explorers from another planet lands on an Earth decimated by a holocaust, but these other-worlders can't quite decipher from the artifacts they find what Earthmen really were like. The visitors wander into Grand Central Station, for example, and find that public washrooms require some kind of tokens for admittance into the stalls. Since they found similar toilet facilities in private homes, which required no such tokens, the interlopers are indeed mystified. The extraterrestrial beings are further confused when they find railway passenger cars marked "Smokers" and "Non-Smokers." They assume that these terms refer to the major racial divisions of the vanished society. In addition, they are utterly perplexed when they discover paintings of angels in an art museum, and assume that there existed a third category of winged Earthmen!

In Arthur Clarke's "History Lesson," Venusians come to an Earth which has been devastated by a great ice age; they find a reel of film which, after many years, they finally learn how to project. The "sleeper" in the story is that while the Venusians think the film portrays the activities of the dominant Earth species, we find at the story's end that what the Venusians actually were watching was a Disney cartoon. This story is a wry comment about many of the assumptions we make about other cultures and sub-cultures which we have reason to study, analyze and, often, make so many judgments about.

Horace Miner's "Body Ritual of the Nacirema" is another interesting story for consideration. Nacirema is "American" spelled backwards, and until students realize this, some of them are completely misled. Medicine cabinets are "charm boxes" and dentists become "holy mouth men" in Nacirema.

Student Response:

When asked if they would mind living in Nacireman society, many students reply with an emphatic "No!" Too infrequently are students called upon to step outside their own culture and look at their own "bizarre" customs the way an imaginary Martian might. Using this story as a catalyst, we have students bring in as many ads as they can find which appeal to or advertise American body rituals — and they bring in hundreds of them from newspapers, magazines, and T.V. Deodorants, shampoos, hair creams, hair sprays, colognes, perfumes for men and women, shavers, and depilatories are just a few items which can be considered part of our American body rituals.

Why people need so many body rituals becomes a key question here. What kinds of body ritual products do your students use? Why? What appeal is being made in the body ritual ads? Do your students find anything distasteful about the ads? What?

Perceiving the Strangeness of Our Own Culture

Stranger in a Strange Land, by Robert Heinlein, gives us one further way of viewing American life. Valentine Michael Smith, born of Earth parents but raised on Mars, is brought to Earth at the age of 18. Some hilarious and touching scenes result as Mike struggles with Earth ways. Mike takes all language literally, for example; so we ask students to find examples of American phrases which might confuse Smith or any other stranger to our culture. Some examples we have received from the sports pages are:

"Cubs Slaughter Cards"; "Hawks Maul Bruins." One student brought in a sports headline from a local paper which proclaimed: "Immaculate Conception Stopped." (The reference was to a rivalry between two basketball teams.) Other phrases students have found are: "You kill me," and "He's my bosom buddy." Students can find scores of confusing phrases, and enjoy doing it.

In Mike's Martian world, a kind of cannibalism was practiced: it was a great honor to eat one's friend when he died. Needless to say, some students find this custom repulsive; so have students analyze their own taboos, which all cultures certainly have. Although students may gasp at the idea of eating dog meat, they have no compunction about eating lamb, cattle, or pig flesh. What is the most sacrilegious thing your students can think of? Why is it particularly sacrilegious? Ask students to remember that sacrilege has much broader connotations than religion.

Because of his Martian frame of reference, Mike also has a terrible time understanding most Earth customs. Consequently, we have students explore situations in which they might have difficulty explaining their customs to a stranger. Ask someone, for example, to explain the game of baseball to an imaginary Arab, who has never even heard of the game. What information should be included? What should be left out? Are the vendors who sell beer and popcorn a part of the game? Explain the principle of a Yo-Yo to an Eskimo. Explain the concept of a corner to a boy who has grown up in a lighthouse and has no understanding of an angle. Explain the concepts of north, south, east, and west to a stranger who knows nothing about the cardinal points of a compass. Keep in mind that people actually exist who have no such directions. Are these exercises too fantastic? We'll never forget reading about a native from the Panamanian jungles who, when first confronted with elevators, thought the floors were moving. Like this man, all of us have had to learn how to perceive.

The teacher might consider concluding this chapter by viewing the film, Planet of the Apes. In the movie, humans are thrust into a subservient relationship with apes — a relationship which results in the humans' being caged, hunted for sport, chained, bred, and experimented upon by the apes. All of these activities may cause students to experience some emotional pangs, but what better way can there be of forcing them to view their own culture?

Exercises in Creativity:

• Have students write original science fiction stories in which they view some American ritual, institution, custom, or invention the way a Martian might. How, for example, might a Martian view the following:

1. The morning rush hour?
2. Sunbathing on the beach?
3. An American funeral?
4. A rodeo?
5. A telephone booth?
6. A supermarket?
7. Television?
8. A drive-in movie or restaurant?
9. A football game?
10. A beauty shop?
11. An American wedding?
12. A hamburger stand?
13. A classroom?
14. Christmas shopping?

• Have students browse through major magazines for examples of ethnocentrism in advertisements and cartoons. Frequently, for example, residents of the Middle East are shown coasting through the air on flying carpets or loping along on camels. Students have found Russians portrayed, with boring consistency, as criminal or gangster types, and Latin Americans as bandidoes. Obviously, these cartoons do a disservice to the complexities of the cultures in question; both teacher and students probably will be amazed at the number of ethnocentric cartoons, in particular, the students can find.

• Have students read travel brochures to see how different countries are described. Words like "exotic," "romantic," and "mysterious" invariably are used in reference to India. Many Indians would be incredulous at this description. Ask students to keep journals of the kinds of descriptive adjectives they find employed for other cultures. What kinds of images are used in describing India, Japan, Africa, the Middle East? Do students think these descriptions are accurate?

• Have students write down, in a free-association exercise, all the images and words that come to mind when the teacher mentions "India," or "Russia," or whatever country the class is studying. With regularity beyond belief, for example, students describe Russia in terms of Dr. Zhivago: cold, fur hats, ice, etc. This exercise should, of course, be done at the beginning of a unit.

Have students make drawings of a "typical" Japanese, Chinese, Indian.

If a complete stranger to our culture should come to the student's home, what 10 things which best represent America would he show him? Why? What five foods, which best represent the United States, would the student serve?

If the student could take the stranger to any place in the U.S.A., where would he take him and why?

Bibliography

Asimov, Isaac, The Caves of Steel, Fawcett.

————, I, Robot, Fawcett.

————, "The Ugly Little Boy," Tomorrow's Children, Isaac Asimov (ed.), Doubleday; also in The Worlds of Science Fiction, Robert Mills (ed.), Paperback Library.

Boulle, Pierre, Planet of the Apes, Signet.

Bradbury, Ray, "All Summer in a Day," Tomorrow's Children, Isaac Asimov (ed.), Doubleday.

Carr, Carol, "Look, You Think You've Got Troubles," A Pocketful of Stars, Damon Knight (ed.), Doubleday; also in Orbit 5, Damon Knight (ed.), Berkley.

Clarke, Arthur, "History Lesson," Expedition to Earth, Harcourt Brace; also in Science Fiction: The Future, Dick Allen (ed.), Harcourt Brace Jovanovich.

Davidson, Avram, "Now Let Us Sleep," The Worlds of Science Fiction, Robert Mills (ed.), Paperback Library.

Heinlein, Robert, Stranger in a Strange Land, Berkley.

Huxley, Aldous, Brave New World, Bantam.

Miner, Horace, "Body Ritual of the Nacirema," A Stress Analysis of a Strapless Evening Gown, Robert Baker (ed.), Doubleday Anchor; also in Apeman, Spaceman, Leon Stover and Harry Harrison (eds.), Berkley.

Nevins, Larry, "The Jigsaw Man," Dangerous Visions, Harlan Ellison (ed.), Berkley.

Simak, Clifford, City, Ace.

Szilard, Leo, "Report on Grand Central Terminal," The Voice of the Dolphin and Other Stories, Simon and Schuster.

Wilson, Richard, "See Me Not," World's Best Science Fiction: Fourth Series, Donald Wollheim and Terry Carr (eds.), Ace.

Chapter 9

SLICING THE PIE: FUTURE ECONOMIC TRENDS
Bringing Economic Principles into Focus

High school economics courses often present either dreary vistas in which supply and demand chase each other up and down endless hills of graph paper, or embody a strictly practical examination of installment buying, banking, and how to be a wise consumer. The practical course can arouse student interest, but it often leads to frustration in economics teachers who long to discuss the differences between Milton Friedman and Walter Heller. It also avoids presenting the theoretical so completely that college-bound students may have a right to be angry about their high school preparation when they are exposed to the university's economics 101. Theoretical economics, on the other hand, is academically respectable — and almost guaranteed to put students to sleep. In addition, neither approach is certain to examine other vital economic issues such as the viability of the American economic system or the question of what that system's future may be.

Science fiction does not adapt too well to the examination of standard micro-economic topics such as supply and demand schedules, the balance of payments problem, or economic growth. The genre _is_ invaluable, however, for any understanding of the broad economics picture; this chapter will explain how Sf can be used to bring parts of that picture into clear focus. Science fiction's primary value in the study of economics is in showing us where, in the opinion of the writer, certain features of the contemporary American economic system may lead in the future. It also should be noted here that, due to the nature of the genre, no bright futures are predicted; after all, problems make better stories than peace or contentment. Remember, too, that we do not recommend at any point in this book that the topics discussed should be approached _solely_ through science fiction. Other materials will, of course, need to be used by the teacher to provide the proper balance; this balance especially may be necessary when the Sf used is sharply critical of present-day American institutions, as is the case in many of the stories cited in this chapter.

Living in a "Throw-Away" Society

Capitalism itself has come under sharp attack by Sf writers, many of whom have been dissecting it for years. One of the neatest pieces of surgery is performed by John Jakes in "The Sellers of the Dream." This story depicts a world dominated by a pair of corporate giants which finally are shown to be merely two branches of the same company. Planned obsolescence is in evidence everywhere, and children whose reading primers are written by the advertising agency B.B.D.& O. are unlikely to rebel against it. The American woman gets not only a new fashion look every year, but a new personality as well — acquired in just a few expensive minutes at the local personality alteration center. A human prototype for the new personality is chosen, or created, each year, but for this woman, the personality change must be permanent. When the model year changes, the living prototype becomes obsolete.

Student Response:

Ask students how concentrated has business already become in America? Although students can look up the latest figures on the size of the top 500 corporations in Fortune, we think it is far better to personalize the student's first realization that a few huge companies dominate our lives. This realization can be achieved by having students keep a record of everything they consume (not just by eating it) in the course of a day, and then tracking down the producers. How many times will names like Du Pont crop up?

Throwing away personalities like used clothing appears to us to be going too far, but the people of Jakes' world are forced to go along with it. Anyone who resists the planned obsolescence of any product, including personalities, or who expresses disapproval of the corporate manipulation of the American people, is considered deviant; deviants are exiled to the prison island of Manhattan, surrounded in the story by huge rat-infested dumps and the poisonous waters of the Hudson River. Jakes' hero is a corporation spy who accidentally discovers that the two dominant companies are really just one big corporation, and that the personality division is trying to mold the girl he loves into the prototype of the coming year's "new personality."

Although the teacher may consider "The Sellers of the Dream" to be too lengthy for classroom use, this story is effective in asking students to consider whether they really want to live in what Alvin Toffler calls, in Future Shock, a "throw-away society." Ask students: how many cars has your family owned in the past 10 years? How many major appliances? In short, just how close are we right now to the kind of society Jakes is attacking? The teacher might wish to read Chapter 4 of Future Shock to gain some greater insights into this problem, or to assign this chapter to a few able students to read. Students can be asked to separate from the weekly trash every item which has been used just once. Does our throwing away so many material things have any implications for the non-material, such as friendships? We have asked seniors how many of them still regard as a good friend the person they felt closest to in the 8th grade; predictably, the number is small. Are Americans better able to adjust to transience in jobs as a result of being trained throughout their lives to throw away things? Do any of your students still admire the same rock singers who were their favorites two years ago? Send your students out on a scavenger hunt to try to find items that were popular in the early 1960s; we suspect that they will have trouble coming up with such things as a Yo Yo, a hula hoop, a "super" ball, or a clip-on bow tie. How long does the number one-rated pop song remain number one? How long does it stay in the "Top 10"? What kinds of products normally are rented rather than purchased? If students don't know the answer to this question, send them to the local rent-all store, or to the yellow pages to find out.

Although planned obsolescence is an easy target, it also can be seen in a favorable light. Economists tell us that a consistently high rate of economic growth brings prosperity; this means that demand must stay high. After all, if things last forever, there will be no reason to replace them. Never mind, however, the implications of unnecessary consumption of increasingly scarce resources. After all, what's more important — ecology or economy? While Detroit hails record automotive production figures, let the auto graveyards encroach like malignant growths on the few green areas left in our major cities. Watch the natural gas producers advertise their products on the one hand, and decry the nation's fuel shortages on the other! Let us also take note of those who sell us what we don't want in order to satisfy the needs we don't know we have — the advertising men.

Advertising and Economic Stability

It must be admitted, of course, that without advertisers to create demand, the penalty suffered by a producer for misreading the public taste would be unsold surplusage; and unconsumed products signal an end to economic growth and, perhaps, the beginning of recession. Seen in this light, advertising plays a vital role in the maintenance of economic stability, but it is, nevertheless, difficult to suppress vague feelings of disquiet when one contemplates some of the methods used by the men from Madison Avenue.

Max Schulman has given the advertising industry a wildly comic treatment in Rally Round the Flag, Boys; Vance Packard, in his famous book The Hidden Persuaders, exposes advertisers who uncover our hidden motivations through psychological probing techniques — then design sales methods which will send us in eager droves to the stores, credit cards in hand.

The first science fiction writers to use advertising as a theme were Frederik Pohl and C. M. Kornbluth, who published The Space Merchants in the early 1950s. Although the main thrust of this book is directed at the advertising industry, the authors also launch many a penetrating salvo against other segments of future America. They envision a U.S. in which a serious housing and water shortage has developed; bicycles have replaced cars in congested urban areas; and anyone who ventures into city streets without soot plugs for his nostrils is not likely to survive long.

McCarthyism was still very much a part of the American scene when The Space Merchants was written, but the subversive menace of the future, as Pohl and Kornbluth see it, will be "Consies" (short for consumers) rather than Commies. As the book begins, its hero, an advertising copy writer, hates and fears the "Consies" as much as anyone else does — for his whole privileged way of life would be

116

destroyed if the lower classes were permitted to buy only what they need. Furthermore, if products were of good quality, they would last longer and thus reduce the demand for replacements. The "Consies" have even gone so far as to advocate the removal of addictive substances from coffee and cigarettes. This, of course, would be too much! Who, after all, would drink 12 cups of coffee a day, and keep a pot by the bed at night, if it were not for the mild alkaloid the coffee contains? What would happen to the coffee industry, and the jobs it provides, if it no longer were possible to get hooked on caffeine elixir?

The hero's view of the world undergoes some changes when he is forced by a "Consie" plot to live for a time as a lower-class consumer. The conclusion of the book finds him in control of a giant advertising agency, prepared to frustrate its attempt to take over and exploit the planet Venus. Instead, he plans to spearhead a quiet movement for Consumerism.

Student Response:

Aside from its biting satire, the strength of The Space Merchants is that many of its projections of 20th Century American society don't look very outlandish any more. It should be easy for students to see where facts nearly have caught up with the book's fiction. Ask students, for example, to name people they know who are addicted to harmful substances like coffee or cigarettes. Have students analyze advertisements and look at TV commercials to determine the source of their appeal. If your school has access to a videotape recorder, so that the whole class can be exposed to the same commercial at the same time, the conditions for this analysis would be ideal, but home sets will serve the purpose. What propaganda techniques (amorphous but glittering generalities, "just plain folks," bandwagons, etc.) are evident in these commercials? If students don't know the names of these techniques, simply have them try to pinpoint the source of each commercial's sales appeal.

Have students watch the Saturday morning cartoons and count, during a two-hour span, the number of commercials which obviously are aimed at children. When some of the best corporate brains in the land are pitted against a 7-year-old's sales resistance, who is going to win? How many students have heard their younger brothers and sisters sing sales jingles or demand that parents buy them products first seen in a TV commercial? Is it clear to students how we are trained almost from birth to be good consumers? How big a step is it, from pleading with parents for the latest Mattel miracle, to hungering after the biggest TV screen and the newest car on the block?

Student Reaction to Materialism

If students question whether anyone really places such strong emphasis on consumption as the foregoing paragraphs indicate, assign them to watch the television program, "Let's Make a Deal." If you haven't seen this program yourself recently, it might be a good idea to look at it again — but be prepared for an uncomfortable bit of self-insight. Giant "carrots" (in reality, members of the audience who have dressed in outlandish costumes to get the attention of the M.C. — and, therefore, to get an opportunity to get on the program and "make a deal") writhe in ecstasy when the M. C. beckons them forward, and hurl themselves into convulsions when they win prizes. It is hard for even the most non-materialistic viewer not to get caught up in the excitement — and enjoy vicariously the naked greed exhibited by both contestants and members of the audience. Ask students what accounts for the appeal of "Let's Make a Deal"? How many commercials are shown on the program, including the plugs for the products given away?

To provide still another example of how thoroughly we have been sold on owning things just for the sake of owning them, the teacher might try to find out how many useless or unnecessary gadgets are owned by students and/or their parents. Ask students why they bought these objects. How many of their personal possessions could students comfortably dispense with? How many of the girls have owned Barbie dolls? (Did you know that it is possible to get a trade-in when the old Barbie begins to wear out and the owner wants a new Barbie?) Often appearing on the back page of the Sunday magazine supplements are small ads for products which are, to say the least, unique. Similar ads can be found in many monthly magazines. The teacher might have a contest to see who can find the ad for the strangest or most useless product. Does the production, advertising, and sale of such items, while poverty still exists for many persons in this country, say anything about our nation's priorities?

Before the teacher permits students to get too indignant over what many may see as a perverted system of national priorities governing the use of limited resources, it might be well to be sure that the students understand how a market system like ours regulates the economy. Under this system, production takes place when there is demand; and demand, to be effective, has to be more than desire — it must be backed up by the ability and willingness to pay, or it is meaningless. Thus, the demand of a rich man ultimately translates itself into production for his needs, but the demand of a poor man does not. There is no moral judgment implied here; that's just how it works. Whether or not we should continue to permit it to work this way is, of course, a different question.

Exploitation of Society by Corporations

The Space Merchants concentrates its main fire on the advertising industry, but Pohl and Kornbluth also have written a more broadly-based attack on American institutions, Gladiator-at-Law. We would not suggest that the teacher use both books with this chapter, but either one can be read in a couple of hours and students will not find them difficult. Gladiator-at-Law depicts an America in which a few great corporations dominate everything and viciously exploit the rest of society in every conceivable way.

In the world described in Gladiator-at-Law, it is impossible to break a corporate contract; anyone who has the economic security such a contract offers must live in virtual slavery. A man can be fired, however, and if that happens he loses his automatic house and his credit cards, both of which are provided by his employer, and is forced to traverse the crumbling highways to Belly Rave.

Belly Rave once was Belle Reve, a suburb where countless thousands of people fell for the developer's "line" and mortgaged their souls for dream houses that turned into nightmares of poor construction and high taxes. At the time of the story, Belle Reve has become a slum where anarchy is total and juvenile gangs prowl the alleys and vacant lots.

No one goes hungry, of course, because the government is never late with the food allotment; but no one has a job, either, since "little black boxes that can't make a mistake" now perform most productive tasks. Except for the very few persons who try to work at pathetic businesses to make themselves feel useful, there is absolutely no creative outlet in Belly Rave. The well-fed inhabitants don't revolt, however, because they are distracted by circuses in the form of "games" which feature engineered forms of torture and death. These games, the authors suggest, are an outgrowth of the preoccupation with violence which manifests itself in American society today.

It is difficult to think of an economic, political, or social institution which does not take a thorough drubbing at the hands of Kornbluth and Pohl. Court trials, for example, are brief, as testimony is transcribed onto punch cards and fed into jury machines. The stock market has replaced the racetrack as the main attraction for gamblers, and the floor of the exchange swarms with brokers peddling tips to eager bettors on their way to the parimutuel windows ("Hey, bud ... GML is hot today").

Does a Corporate Conscience Exist?

If time does not permit the use of either The Space Merchants or Gladiator-at-Law, Fritz Leiber's "A Bad Day for Sales" (cited in Chapter 6) can be used to raise at least one of the points made by Pohl and Kornbluth: is there any such thing as a corporate conscience? The indictment of capitalism implied in this story may not be the major theme of the work, but it certainly is present. Is this kind of extreme attack on "the system" convincing? Is it justified?

At this point it might be well for the teacher to begin blending the thoughts of economists about capitalism with the speculations of Messrs. Kornbluth, Pohl, and Leiber. John Kenneth Galbraith's New Industrial State, as well as certain sections of The Greening of America, by Charles Reich, might appeal to some students. Milton Friedman argues that the only proper function for a businessman in a smoothly functioning economy is to make money; when the businessman develops a social conscience, the Chicago economist argues, he subverts his true function. Friedman's works are not easy reading, but they might provide a bit of needed balance for the teacher, if not for the students. Galbraith and Reich, of course, argue for a business structure more responsive to social problems; the economic reasoning behind these opposing positions could be explored by students at this point.

According to Walter Rostow, the American economy is nearly past the stage in which its organization is for the highest possible level of production. Services loom ever larger in the GNP figures as the demand for goods approaches satiation. When everyone has enough of everything, what then? How can the economy continue to grow and to stave off a surplus-induced depression? Again, Frederik Pohl provides us with an answer, this time in "The Midas Plague."

Forcing People to Consume Goods

In this story, Pohl hilariously reverses most of the cherished values of our Puritan ancestors and, by so doing, creates a world that many readers may, at first, think sounds like paradise. The American economic machine continues to grind out products at an ever-increasing rate; since the government does not know how to stop production without causing a terrible depression, everyone is required — by law — to consume. Those with the lowest incomes are required to consume the most; to live in the largest mansions, spend the largest liquor allowances, buy the most cars, etc. Being able to let someone else buy you a drink is a sign of higher status, and if you are lucky enough to advance to grade four, you may be allowed to move into a small house and use only one or two refrigerators, washing machines, wardrobes, etc. each year. The obvious solution for those who get tired of caviar seven days a week is simply to throw it out, but deliberate waste is forbidden. The story's hero finally develops a method of increasing his consumption without wasting anything and, therefore, is hailed as a national savior.

When consumption becomes more important than production, businesses naturally will increase their advertising pressure long before the government is forced to create a ration board to enforce consumption, as in "The Midas Plague." If the surplus grows too large, subliminal advertising might appear, even though it is against the law. This is the theme of "Subliminal Man," by J. G. Ballard.

121

As in "The Midas Plague," the government in
Ballard's story does all it can to force people to consume.
The characters in "The Midas Plague," however, live in
what we would consider luxury and receive their consumption
quotas at no charge. They suffer only from obesity, caused
by the required 12-course meals, and fatigue brought on by
the grind of constant consuming. In "Subliminal Man," the
goods must be paid for, so most people have to work at
more than one job and are entrapped by endless payments.

Student Response:

If it can be done without embarrassing individuals,
a very instructive project for this chapter is to have students
find out just how many installment payments their own families
make each month. What household items have been bought on
time payments? In some affluent suburbs, it is not uncommon
to find students who have their own charge accounts, or who
are making payments on motorcycles or cars. How many
students believe in paying cash for major purchases? Experience suggests that there will be very few who act in
accordance with such a belief, although a number may profess it. The previous questions have implied, perhaps, that
there is something wrong with the extensive use of credit;
students should not hesitate to question this view.

In "Subliminal Man," products are standardized so
that there is only one brand of everything, and quality is
uniformly low. This uniformity certainly would be technically efficient, but the respected scholar Arnold Toynbee
argues that we already pay a high price for this efficienty
in terms of reduced choice of goods. Further technological advances, he argues, will bring even more uniformity,
until finally we will have no freedom of choice at all. It
would appear, however, that Toynbee's view conflicts
directly with the trend now evident, which is not "no choice"
but, in Alvin Toffler's words, "overchoice."

The question of whether we are moving toward standardization or overchoice is one that easily can be investigated by students. They can visit the supermarket and return with lists of names (and sizes of) all the different detergents, cleansers, cigarettes, and beans found on the shelves. When the students' grandparents were in their teens, was there more choice or less on grocery store shelves? Assign a few students to take the 1900 Sears-Roebuck catalog (now readily available) and, being sure to look at products which have not gone out of use, compare it with a current catalog. Ask other students to do the same project using a 10-year-old catalog, if one can be found. The results will immediately be apparent — it is overchoice, not uniformity, which increasingly confronts us. Ask students to put together a page or two of a Sears catalog that may be published in the year 2000.

The Consequences of Overchoice

Is there anything dangerous about being able to choose from such a bewildering variety of products? In other words, just what are the probable consequences of overchoice? When there are many similar products on the market, what form is competition likely to take? Once again the teacher might assign the relevant chapter from Future Shock to the better students, or read it himself for some ideas about the possible results of overchoice. Another valuable exercise for students to undertake might be to visit some local car dealers and discover the range of options available in a given model. Students will find that "there have been some changes made" since the days when one could buy any style of Model A one chose, as long as it was a black sedan!

Stories like "Subliminal Man" and "The Midas Plague" readily lend themselves to consideration of a possible economic future in which the emphasis is on consumption rather than production. Obviously, the two aspects are interrelated — as the old song puts it, "you can't have one without the other." This is why economics teachers are fond of drawing on the chalkboard complex charts depicting the flow of goods and services between producers and consumers. Unfortunately, it is not at all unusual for a student to make the mistake of thinking that some people produce and others consume; when the teacher detects this error, he must point out that, in reality, everyone is both producer and consumer. The chart which makes it look as if production and consumption are the prerogative of separate groups is simply a handy way of explaining how individuals play different economic roles, and how a market economy operates.

Basing an Economy on War Materiel

In the society depicted by Theodore Cogswell in "Consumer's Report," however, consumers and producers are members of separate classes. The class separation described by Cogswell came about when the society recognized that it was drowning in surplus products. To get rid of this surplus, the authorities decided to channel the nation's resources into war goods, which are consumed very quickly. Perhaps because it was unable to find any "inferior" races to absorb the bombs and grenades, the government brings about the use of this war materiel on the home front, by creating a class division between adults — who produce the weapons — and children — who consume them. Small cowboys and Indians carry real guns; grenade samples arrive in the mail; and the big game at the stadium is fought from foxholes with mortars and rifles. Children who manage to grow up must undergo reconditioning to make them forget their consumer roles; then they become producers, and raise little consumption units of their own. The reconditioning process is thorough: no one ever questions the justice of the arrangement — this kind of life is just the "way things are."

Student Response:

Suppose international tensions were eliminated or reduced; what would be the effect of the resultant cuts in the defense budget on our nation's economy? How high might our unemployment figures jump? What areas of the country would be the hardest hit by such a decision? If war goods were eliminated from the figures for GNP, how much would our GNP fall? In short, is this story really as far-fetched as it first appears? Does the economic well-being of our nation also rest on weapons production?

Some students may be more than ready to condemn the entire American economic system as being dominated by the rich, dependent on war for stability, and oppressive of the poor. If this is how it is, some may say, then let's change the system.

Choosing a Workable System

Political and economic theorists have been trying to figure out for centuries just what the "system" should be like, if it were to be changed, but they have reached no agreement. Pure capitalism, of course, never has been tried, nor has a "pure" anything else. Among the suggestions offered repeatedly by various soothsayers as the ideal type of economic organization is some form of utopian socialism. This sytem has not been any more successful than pure capitalism, but writers are fond of describing what they believe might happen in some future time if the dreams of the utopians should come true.

The utopia theme has, in fact, long been one of the special provinces of writers of science fiction. It is also true, however, that many who have chosen this theme have been social critics with axes to grind rather than polished writers. Edward Bellamy, for example, wrote his famous Looking Backward as a criticism of 19th Century society. The same may be said of Erewhon, by Samuel Butler. A modern example is Walden II, by the famous bevarioralist B. F. Skinner. If the reader is able to accept the implications of behavioral engineering, Skinner probably offers a better prescription, than anyone else, for an utopia that is capable of realization. Skinner, however, tends to let his main character do a good deal of lecturing, which many high school students would not bother to read. None of the works mentioned so far has a great deal of literary merit, but they all can present an alternative against which to measure capitalism.

All of the utopias mentioned so far are seen by their authors as Edens, created to show the rest of us how things ought to be. Mack Reynolds, in "Utopian," gives us another view — one of a world which has completely solved the problems of war, race relations, crime, and pollution, but which has one fatal flaw. A few people who have recognized the flaw reach back into the past and bring forward one of the conspirators who helped wreck the old society. They hope that, with his revolutionary skills, he can help the new underground find a way to get rid of the dark spot in Eden — even if it means going back to the way things were. The underground believes that man has gone soft. Scientific progress has come to a halt; no one cares about going out into space or climbing mountains because they are there. All dynamism and creativity seems to have vanished, and humanity is stagnating. Men are, as Reynolds puts it, "fighting animals"; once the world's problems were solved and there was nothing left to work for, they became frustrated and unhappy. Thus has utopia, which was designed to free man, enslaved him instead, and perfection is breeding revolution.

Student Response:

The obvious question to ask students about utopias is: what kind of practical difficulties stand in the way of building them? If a utopia could be built, what flaws of its own might it develop? What happened to real utopian experiments such as Brook Farm or New Harmony? Do students think that they themselves would have to change if they were to live in an utopia? Ask the class to create their own perfect world, or have individuals do this through an essay or short story.

Students creating a utopia may have a tendency to concentrate on political and social questions, and gloss over economic issues. If the teacher does not want this oversight to happen, he may have to give students a few guidelines which will stimulate a full development of the economic side of the utopia. How, for example, will the basic economic problem of limited resources and unlimited wants be solved in the student-created utopia? Who will own the means of production? How will distribution of goods and services be handled? Will there be a division of labor? Will they have any kind of a class system?

After students have created their utopias, they might consider, as a final exercise, the specific changes which would have to take place in the American economy to bring these utopias into being. How might the necessary changes be effected? Perhaps the teacher will want the plans for utopias to be exchanged and read; then students can try to explain how the utopias they have just examined might turn into dystopias. In any case, whether America's economic future will be utopia, dystopia, armegeddon, or just business — as usual, science fiction can furnish both teacher and students with the ideal means of exploring that future before it arrives.

Bibliography

Ballard, J. G., "Subliminal Man," Eco-Fiction, John Stadler (ed.), Washington Square Press.

Bellamy, Edward, Looking Backward, Lancer.

Butler, Samuel, Erewhon, Signet.

Cogswell, Theodore, "Consumer's Report," Voyages: Scenarios for a Ship Called Earth, Rob Sauer (ed.), Ballantine; also in SF: Author's Choice, Harry Harrison (ed.), Berkley.

Jakes, John, "The Sellers of the Dream," Spectrum #4, Kingsley Amis and Robert Conquest (eds.), Berkley.

Kornbluth, C. M. and Pohl, Frederik, Gladiator-at-Law, Ballantine.

————, The Space Merchants, Ballantine

Leiber, Fritz, "A Bad Day for Sales," Nightmare Age, Frederik Pohl (ed.), Ballantine.

Pohl, Frederik, "The Midas Plague," Nightmare Age, Frederik Pohl (ed.), Ballantine; also in Spectrum, Kingsley Amis and Robert Conquest (eds.), Berkley.

Reynolds, Mack, "Utopian," The Year 2000, Harry Harrison (ed.), Berkley.

Skinner, B. F., Walden II, MacMillan.

Chapter 10

THE VIEW FROM THE 1,000th FLOOR: FUTURE CITIES
Downtown Areas Begin to Decay

If one of the alien beings who have been wandering through these pages were to crank up his time machine and whirl back to the 1970s, he might wonder just how much longer this much-abused planet can endure. Certainly this would be the case if he were to materialize in one of our major cities. Provided he had his respirator handy to help him survive the smog, and if he managed to avoid being run down by snorting vehicles or scurrying humans, he might well conclude that homo sapiens has taken leave of whatever senses he once possessed.

Even a bird does not foul its own nest, but our urban areas are choked with the filth of human occupation. Nowhere else can one see environmental crisis and overpopulation in so virulent a concentration. Mass transit, where it exists at all, shudders regularly to a halt — while fares soar. The city becomes a jungle after dark, and the word "mugger" in a stand-up comic's routine guarantees a bitter laugh. Amidst crumbling walls and ruined streets, black men endure poverty in growing rage while their children chew contentedly on lead-painted plaster. On warm evenings in the ghetto, the moist odor of uncollected garbage turn the stomach of the trembling suburbanite who drives hurriedly through the "bad area." Power failures and brownouts are commonplace events, as are skyrocketing electric bills. Carbon monoxide fumes seep into the brains of traffic-stalled commuters. Full-service department stores move to the suburban shopping centers, and sagging buildings in downtown areas stand empty or are occupied by sleazy bookstores and porno theaters.

Although this may be an overly-dramatic picture of downtown decay, it describes with uncomfortable accuracy the degenerating state of many American cities. This view also reflects the despondency of urban man as he struggles with the city's seemingly-insurmountable problems. Some Sf writers have seen in the future the total decay of cities; others have predicted salvation and transformation. For some, man's future remains among the skyscrapers, but others see his final destiny back on the land, or even among the stars. Obviously, there are many alternative futures for the American city, and we think that Sf is one of the best ways to give students a look at what some of those futures might be.

Perhaps the most logical way to handle the question of what might happen to our cities is to cite a few stories which continue some present trends to the ultimate point. One of the best of these is "Among the Bad Baboons," by Mack Reynolds. This grim tale is laid in nearly-deserted New York, one of the many major cities to be abandoned after a series of great riots. Frightened citizens, who already were flocking to the suburbs, now have abandoned the city altogether. Industry has followed, and the tax revenue from slum property has not been enough to maintain basic city services. The loss of services has driven most of the erstwhile rioters out of town, too, so the only people remaining in the central city are artists, who stubbornly refuse to abandon Greenwich Village, and the baboons — human scavengers who feed on the moldering corpse of the once-proud metropolis. There is no government or law left in the empty city, so those who still hide there exist in a warlike state which is aggravated from time to time by hunters from the suburbs who sneak back to hunt "baboons."

Like Reynolds, Clifford Simak also sees the likelihood of deserted cities in the near future, but he believes that the fear of riots will not cause the abandonment of cities. In "City," Simak explains the decaying cities as the product of technological advances which have made home construction inexpensive, and the switch to hydroponic food production which has put farmers out of business and made land cheap. Since privately-owned helicopters now make transportation easy and fast, most former city residents now are able to acquire that "place in the country" about which so many Americans have dreamed.

In this future time, people can afford simply to walk away from their city homes, leaving them to be occupied by dispossessed farmers, who now exist in bitterness on society's leavings. Only one enterprising individual has been able to adapt to the new reality; he has converted his farm into a tourist attraction. Although city government tries at first to pretend it still has something to do, administrators finally are forced to admit that they have nothing to govern, and they, too, join the exodus to the country.

Inner Cities Are Controlled by Blacks

Even more likely to occur in the future than totally-abandoned cities are nearly all-black cities, particularly if present demographic trends continue. Robert Silverberg, in "Black Is Beautiful," which is set in the year 2000, describes a New York City completely controlled by blacks, many of whom are so satisfied with economic and political power that they no longer seek integration. A few token whites are kept on payrolls by liberal black executives, but even they return at the end of the day by "hopter" to their own suburbs, a hundred miles from the city. On weekends, the only whites in New York are tourists, and the black government encourages their visits because they bring in revenue. Looking at cities like Gary, Newark, Cleveland, and Los Angeles which have elected black mayors, it is easy to see the growing influence of blacks in major cities. Whether the rest of Silverberg's forecast also will prove accurate remains to be seen.

Student Response:

In addition to riots and changing racial characteristics, what other conditions seem likely to prevail in major urban areas by the year 2000? How many of your students would select a large city as a preferred place of residence? What are the reasons for their decision? What changes might make the city more attractive to your students? If your students already live in the city, would they like to move out someday? Why or why not?

We suspect that many students will express dislike for the city and urban living; more than one Sf writer has expressed a similar view, sometimes by describing the city as "a jungle." Reynolds' and Simak's urban jungles are, as we have seen, nearly deserted; Silverberg's city has gone black, and Robert Scheckley's ("The People Trap," cited in Chapter 3) is so packed with people that it takes literally hours for a traveler in a hurry to fight his way a distance of 50 feet. In J. G. Ballard's "Billenium" (cited in Chapter 2), huge "crowd locks," which sometimes last for days, are common.

Consolidation of Suburbs

Rather than deal with the city's problems, many 20th Century Americans have fled to the suburbs — so many of them, in fact, that suburban problems are beginning to look increasingly urban. Some suburbs, for example, now are so crowded that the population approaches in density some of the most congested square blocks in the city. You doubt this? Try driving to a shopping center during a peak period, or try to get a seat in a popular theater on Saturday night. Ask your students to examine modern housing trends in the suburbs. About what percentage of present construction is multiple-family housing? How does this figure compare with one of 10 years ago? When did condominia first appear on the scene? Quadrominia? Are there really many differences between city life and suburban life?

As suburbs grow and begin to overlap, there are moves afoot to consolidate them for the sake of greater efficiency. Might the future see the merging, into vast Megaopoli, of consolidated suburbs with the parent cities? Should the government permit this action? What could be done to prevent it? It has been suggested that relatively empty sections of the United States encourage the migration of city dwellers as a way of easing congestion in urban areas. What would the government have to do to get your students to move to North Dakota?

Although the real differences between city and suburban living may be decreasing, and the future of these areas may lie in consolidation, this future unity generally is not recognized by either suburbanites or city dwellers. In fact, there is a great deal of tension and bad feeling between people who have escaped to suburbia and those trapped by poverty in the inner city. Commuters who work "downtown" use city services, but pay no taxes to help maintain them, and probably shop closer to home. The present antagonism between city dwellers and residents of suburbia, who see themselves as representatives of two separate ways of life, is graphically projected in Fritz Leiber's "X Marks the Pedwalk" (cited in Chapter 5); Robert Silverberg, in "Black Is Beautiful," suggests that growing racial polarization will make these feelings worse.

Antagonism Between City Dwellers and Suburbanites

Possibly the best Sf example of city/suburban antagonism is "Gantlet," by Richard Peck. The city in this story
is a solid mass of buildings, which have been joined together
and sealed to keep out pollution, and ringed by defenses
against the dangerous hordes that live in "Opensky." The
people of "Opensky" are those whom Welfare Control has
judged not worth saving. Some of these people exist on the
dole; a few, of comparatively good character, are allowed
out of "Opensky" into a third circle, "Workring," where
they keep the industries operating. No "skyers," however,
are allowed into the city. "Opensky" people are able to exist
only because the oxygen plants in the city send a metered flow
of life-preserving pure air into the individual bubbles which
surround the "Opensky" dwellings. The "skyers," of course,
resent it when Welfare Control raises the oxygen rates; this
rate increase is just one of the reasons why they hate the
city and constantly try to break in and destroy it.

The city's one potentially vulnerable area is the
tunnel used by the high-speed hovercraft which bring the
daily commuters from 30 miles outside "Workring," where
the privileged classes live. The battered trains, operated
by a commuter co-op since the railroad went bankrupt, must
run a gantlet of bullets and refuse as the bitter residents of
"Opensky" risk automatic lasers and machine guns to mount
their desperate attempts at sabotage.

Suburban Student Response:

If you teach in a suburban school, it might prove interesting to take a poll to find out how long the families of
each of your students have lived outside the city. If you can
find a good map of the metropolitan area, the students can
show, by means of colored pins or yarn, the various places
where their families have lived; thus, the pattern of movement from city to suburb will become clear. What are the
students' attitudes toward the city from which their parents
may have come? It is not at all uncommon to find some
students whose parents have an almost pathological fear and
hatred of the city, and who refuse to let their children go on
field trips into town. We have known students who live within
45 minutes of downtown Chicago, but who know little and care

less about the cultural opportunities offered by the city — and who have never been to the Loop in their lives. What is the reason for their indifference or fear? Have students make a list of things they are afraid of; see how many items on this list are, in some way, related to the city. Is such fear warranted? Ask students to find out, from your local police department, the trend of the crime rate in your suburb. The teacher might improvise a short simulation exercise at this point, in which students are allocated limited amounts of money to build a community. What services will they demand? Which will they be willing to forego? We have found that students will sacrifice almost any other city service for the sake of strong police protection.

The frightened suburbanite can be viewed as a pathetic figure — fleeing the city, he has brought his fear along with him. Have students who doubt this statement look through the yellow pages of a suburban telephone directory and count the ads for security services, locksmiths, and fences. Suburban students also can report on the number of large dogs living in their immediate neighborhoods, and perhaps even on the number of guns kept for protection in their block.

City Student Response:

If your school is a city school, what is the attitude of the students toward the suburbs? Do they reciprocate the hatred and fear felt by many residents of suburbia, or are the suburbs so alien that students don't think about them at all? How many students never have been outside the city? What do they imagine suburbia to be like? Why not arrange a field trip to a suburb, or a student exchange with a suburban school, and give them a chance to find out? Have students draw a map or picture of what they think a typical suburb looks like.

Interdependence of City and Suburb

Some students probably will have difficulty understanding that suburb and city are interdependent and need to attack their problems together. Perhaps it is easiest to see this interdependence in the area of mass transit, where plans encompassing entire metropolitan areas obviously are needed before any effective moving of people can be done. It might be worthwhile, at this point, for the teacher and students to analyze the impact on state and county politics of the flight from city to suburb. Sometimes, are there political reasons why problems are not overcome? Would the consolidation of inefficient local governments result in some politicians losing office? Ask suburban students to explore in depth the problems which would result if the nearest city suddenly should vanish. How would their own lives change? Would their parents still have jobs? Even if the parent's present job is in a suburb, how long would it be before the company decided to relocate closer to a major urban center? In short, do suburban students have a real stake in the existence of a healthy nearby city?

City-dwelling students, of course, do not need to be convinced that it is in their best interests if cities can be made more livable. These students will be familiar with problems of crime, transit, pollution, decaying neighborhoods, etc.; with a little guidance from the teacher and the school, they can begin to organize themselves for action. Have them choose a neighborhood problem and try to solve it by taking whatever action is necessary. Contact the local alderman, call the sanitation department, hold a public meeting, or invite a knowledgeable speaker to the class. Get out and ring doorbells; put pressure on the city government if it becomes necessary to do so. In offering these suggestions, we are again operating on the premise that the school should function as an agent of change, and we are fully aware that not everyone will agree with this view. If either the teacher or the administration believes that classroom work should not extend outside the school building, stress may have to be placed on learning about the problems instead of attacking them directly.

Future Cities and the Need for Privacy

The previous series of stories depicted present-day cities as they could be a few years from now. Assuming that ways can be found to prevent the total dissolution of cities, what might they ultimately become?

Isaac Asimov has given his answer to this question in the previously-discussed book, The Caves of Steel. In this book, the city is underground; in fact, people have developed such a pathological fear of open space that they will leave their warren only in cases of dire need. Food is produced by robots who till the soil on the planet's surface. Transportation in Asimov's city is by expressway, but no one drives on it; the expressway is a giant moving belt made up of lanes of different speeds. Citizens who hold high ratings are entitled to seats on the conveyor belt. Population has mushroomed; when people are outside their small apartments or dormitories, they are expected to observe an elaborate code of etiquette which serves to maintain the illusion of privacy. One may not speak in a public washroom, for example, and it is considered extremely rude to make eye contact with another person.

Student Response:

What are the norms and values of Asimov's society? How are these values shaped by the city's congestion? How has this city solved some of the problems which beset us today?

In sharp contrast to Asimov's mole world is Robert Silverberg's future city in The World Inside (cited in Chapter 3), which soars for 1,000 stories. Within this huge structure most men live their entire lives, happily, but with no privacy at all. Even a wish to be alone is considered deviant; nudity is common, although in The Caves of Steel, it would have been unheard of.

By using both of these books in class, students can compare two possible urban futures. Which of them sounds more appealing to your students? Do both views of the future sound impossible? Yet, shortly before his death in 1959, Frank Lloyd Wright was planning a mile-high building; and much of our country's defense command structure is buried inside mountains at the present time.

In The World Inside, it is not only privacy which is lacking, but also the institution of private property and a sense of real "rootedness." According to Bruno Bettelheim's study of young people raised on an Israeli kibbutz, the need to possess is so important that the children of the kibbutz began to identify with trees and land features when they were deprived of most other possessions.

The teacher who probes the childhood memories of his students, perhaps by having them write autobiographies, often discovers that they remember things like rocks or prairies which they thought of, in childhood, as "theirs." Ask students if, in constructing a world in which people are generally content despite the fact that they have almost no private property, Silverberg has given sufficient consideration to Bettelheim's work? Ask students to write a story in which they explain how and why the first of Silverberg's urbmons was constructed, or to tell of the changes a visitor from 20th Century America would have to make if he were to live in Asimov's underground city.

Learning to "Operate" A Large City

As our cities grow larger, they become increasingly impossible to operate. How, for example, can traffic be kept moving when "expressways" are obsolete as soon as they are opened? As the growing number of power outages in many major cities has shown, it is getting harder for utilities to stand the strain placed on them during peak hours. Almost every major mass transit system in the U.S. is in deep trouble. In some cities, dialing a telephone number is a new kind of roulette: callers gamble that their call will be the one to get past the telephone company's overloaded circuits. Must we invent a totally new type of city if we hope to keep cities alive, or is there a way to make big cities work?

J. G. Ballard describes one way to operate a large city successfully in his story, "Chronopolis." The city in "Chronopolis" has been abandoned, however, as a result of a mass revolt against the devices used to make it operable. Before the revolution, the entire population of the city was on shifts, with each shift assigned to a specific color. Every week the city fathers published a giant schedule which revealed which colors would be permitted to engage in a long list of activities during the coming week. All blues, for instance, would leave work at a certain time and be permitted to shop, eat lunch, and make telephone calls only at certain hours during the week. In order to be sure that no one could disrupt the system by inadvertently violating the time schedules, huge clocks were erected all over the city, each keyed to the master clock on the city hall.

Naturally, a system like that described in "Chronopolis" could be used to give some classes ultra privileges and to discriminate against others (how would your students like their grocery shopping time to be from 3:00 to 3:30 a.m., but their work day to end at 5:00 p.m.?). This time-clock system finally drove the people of Ballard's city to revolt. After the successful revolution, the people banned all clocks and watches as symbols of tyranny, and learned to get along very well without them.

Student Response:

Would a system of carefully-timed shifts, such as Ballard's, effectively regulate a city's operation? How would students like to live in a city run in this manner? How dependent are they now on precise timing? If students normally wear a watch, ask them to go without it for a week. The teacher also might cover the classroom clock and see what happens. Will students ask to have it uncovered? Will they begin to grow restive by instinct when only five minutes remain in the class period? Does the school operate on a shift system to ease overcrowding? If it does, how might the unusual school hours affect homelife, job choice, school clubs, health, etc.? Ask students to keep a 7-day time journal, in which they record exactly what they were doing each half hour of the entire week. Will they find that they are doing the same thing at nearly the same time just about every day?

Overcoming An Obsession with Time and a Fear of Computers

People from other cultures often think that Americans are obsessed with being "on time," and perhaps we are. The ultimate extension of such an obsession, and a telling argument against adopting the system of "Chronopolis" to make our cities function, is found in Harlan Ellison's prize-winning "'Repent, Harlequin,' Said the Ticktockman" (cited in Chapter 7). In this story, the government carefully tallies up each person's late minutes; when the man who somehow can't be on time accumulates a specified number of minutes, his life is cancelled like a postage stamp.

It may be, of course, that we will not have to make the people adjust to the city in order to get the city to work, for this is an area in which the intelligent use of computers might serve us well. If human error can be eliminated from traffic control techniques, for example, more cars can be accommodated — without long delays — during peak traffic periods. Police officers of the future might be robots, programmed to enforce city ordinances and linked to a central computer which also would run other city services. The catch in planning a fully-computerized city, however, might be the fact that computers have brains, but no sense — a point explored more fully in Chapter 4. Some cities already use computers for various operations: part of Chicago's expressway system, for example, utilizes sensing devices, buried in the pavement, to measure the flow of traffic and automatically adjust the interval of stoplights permitting access to the road. Do students know of other ways in which cities are beginning to use computer technology to streamline their operations? Do advances in this field offer some real hope to cities of the present as well as those of the future?

Portrait of a "Living" City:

From the computer-run city, which operates in
purely mechanical fashion but still is under human control,
it is only a step to "Single Combat," by Robert Abernathy.
Here, the city is alive, and is so determined to preserve
itself that it traps, and finally kills, a man who is a threat
to its existence. No one is likely to accept the idea of a
living city, now or in the future, but "Single Combat" presents such a finely-drawn portrait of a great urban cancer
that it might cause readers to stop and ask if this kind of
blight is what we really want. The city's wretched victim
might, perhaps, stand for all city dwellers who are trapped
in a way of life from which escape seems impossible.

Student Response:

Ironically, there may be no real reason to stay
trapped. Are cities really necessary? Can modern technology, applied to transportation and communication, make
cities obsolete? Why did these congested areas grow up in
the first place? Are the circumstances that produced cities
still present? Ask students to design a livable city, or to
explain how we might be able to get rid of cities altogether.
Some students should be encouraged to cut loose from present
technological limitations when designing their cities, but
others should be asked to stay within them.

Speculative Views of the City of the Far-Distant Future

To conclude this chapter, and remembering that one
of the most important uses for science fiction is to spark
creativity, we suggest the use of several stories which carry
the theme of man and the city into distant millenia — so distant, in fact, that some students may have trouble following
them.

One of the most speculative views of the city of the
far-distant future is found in "Build-Up," by the highly-
gifted J. G. Ballard. In this story, the city is completely
underground, and is built upon many levels. It is so complex that no one knows the entire city; nor can anyone remember any other way of life. Because the city is very
crowded, all of its space must be used; there is no such

thing as non-functional space here. Space is sold by the cubic foot; if a citizen wishes to gain title to a cubic foot of air, he must buy it. The city obviously has existed for thousands of years, for birds have evolved into a wingless form. While the city has rail transportation, airplanes are unknown. The story's hero discovers the principle of the airplane, but can find no place where there is enough open space to fly one. He sets out, therefore, to discover where the city ends — only to return, finally, to his starting point. Obviously, the whole planet is circumvented by one gigantic city. How has this city solved some of the problems facing our cities today? What different problems does it have?

E. M. Forster, in "The Machine Stops," also envisions underground cities for the future, although there is still air transportation on the planet's surface in his story. In the distant time of which he writes, there is no population problem because reproduction is infrequent. People live like bees in a giant honeycomb, one person to a cell; isolated underground, each man is cared for by the great machine which runs everything. It is normal for a man to communicate with others, deliver lectures, and seek new ideas — all without leaving the security of his own room. People do not live particularly well because the machine has standardized everything at a low level for its own convenience; communication facilities and other machine-provided services are "just good enough." Everyone is patient, however, while they wait for the machine to repair its failing circuits and to improve conditions. Ostensibly, there is no religion, but the instruction manual describing how to use the machine is a much-revered book, and worship of the machine gradually is growing. Physical strength is an undesirable characteristic; those who are unfortunate enough to be relatively strong — able, perhaps, to hold a pillow at arm's length for as long as a minute — are weeded out as being deviant. Also deviant, of course, is anyone who is not content to remain in his cell, but who actually wishes to travel in person or to have face-to-face contact with other human beings.

The climax of the story comes when one man decides to visit the outside world without obtaining the required egress permit. He discovers that the deviants previously exiled to the planet's surface have not perished, as everyone had expected. Finally, the machine grinds to a halt, and the future of Earth is left to those who still survive aboveground.

The "machine becomes God" or the "machines are unreliable" themes of this story qualify "The Machine Stops" for inclusion in Chapter 4 as well as here. Surely, however, this entire concept of a city is so completely alien that it must be considered in a chapter on future cities or in a creativity unit.

Student Response:

What are the norms and values of this beehive world? If a citizen of this city came to live in your town, what adjustments would he have to make? How might you and the visitor misunderstand each other? If the visitor were to take you back to his city, what adjustments would you have to make? What problems now existing in American cities would be solved if we lived in cities such as the one described in "The Machine Stops"? What new problems, which Forster has not mentioned, might this kind of city create?

As a final assignment, the teacher might suggest the writing of a story in which students try to predict the future of the city as a form of human organization. Some students might be encouraged to read Arthur Clarke's 2001: A Space Odyssey and then be asked to deal with an even broader question — not, simply, what is the future of cities, but what is the ultimate destiny of man?

Bibliography

Abernathy, Robert, "Single Combat," Cities of Wonder, Damon Knight (ed.), Macfadden-Bartell.

Asimov, Isaac, The Caves of Steel, Fawcett Crest.

Ballard, J. G., "Billenium," Voyages: Scenarios for a Ship Called Earth, Rob Sauer (ed.), Ballantine.

———, "Build-Up," Connoisseurs of SF, Tom Boardman (ed.), Penguin.

———, "Chronopolis," Chronopolis and Other Stories, Berkley.

Ellison, Harlan, "'Repent, Harlequin,' Said the Ticktockman," Social Education, February, 1973; also in Nebula Award Stories, 1965, Damon Knight (ed.), Doubleday; and Tenth Galaxy Reader, Frederik Pohl (ed.), Doubleday.

Forster, E. M., "The Machine Stops," Cities of Wonder, Damon Knight (ed.), Macfadden-Bartell.

Leiber, Fritz, "X Marks the Pedwalk," Nightmare Age, Frederik Pohl (ed.), Ballantine.

Peck, Richard, "Gantlet," Orbit #10, Damon Knight (ed.), Berkley.

Reynolds, Mack, "Among the Bad Baboons," Nightmare Age, Frederik Pohl (ed.), Ballantine; also in Eleventh Galaxy Reader, Frederik Pohl (ed.), Doubleday.

Scheckley, Robert, "The People Trap," The Best from Fantasy and Science Fiction, 18th Series, Edward L. Ferman (ed.), Ace.

Silverberg, Robert, "Black Is Beautiful," The Year 2000, Harry Harrison (ed.), Berkley.

———, The World Inside, Signet.

Simak, Clifford, "City," City, Ace.

———, "Day of Truce," Nightmare Age, Frederik Pohl (ed.), Ballantine.

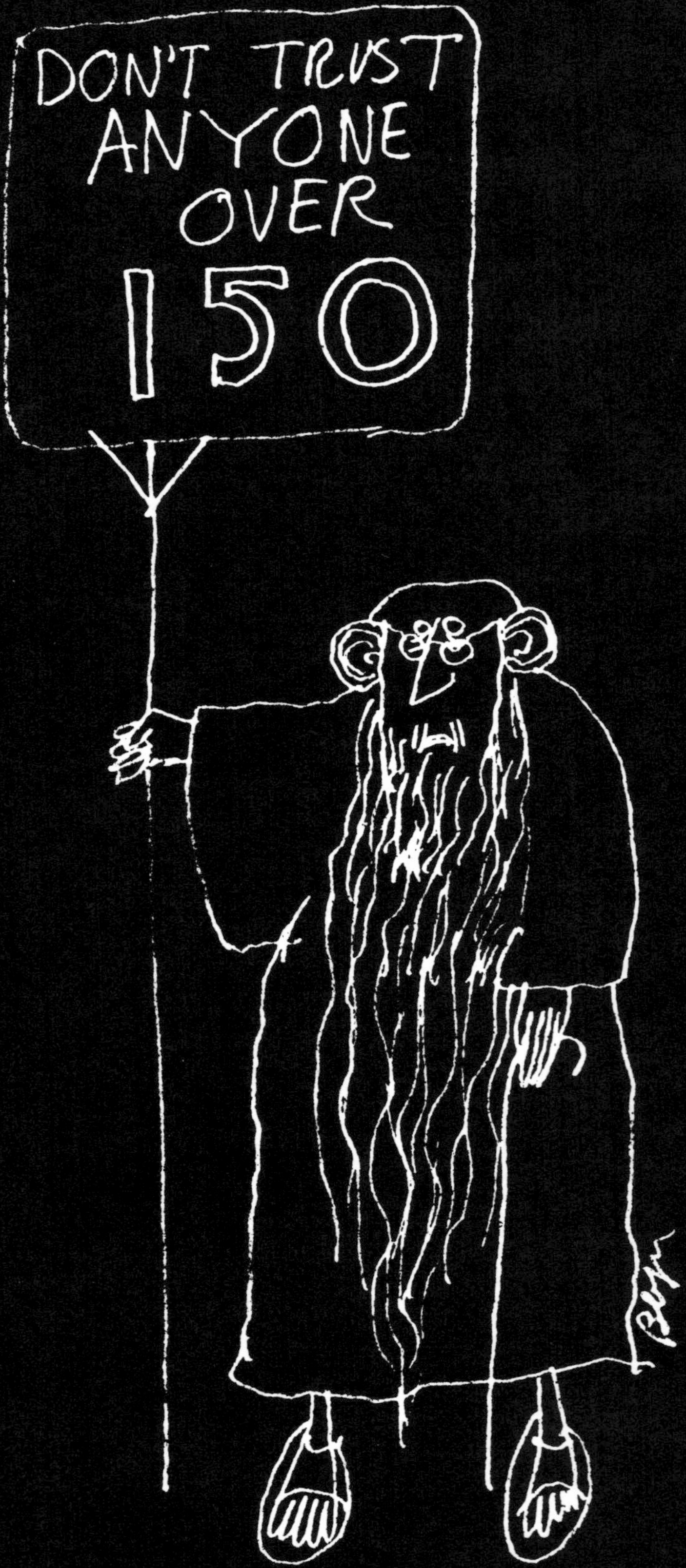
DON'T TRUST ANYONE OVER 150

Chapter 11

DON'T TRUST ANYONE OVER 150: THE GENERATIONS
Age Stratification Overcomes Social Interaction

Is there a generation gap — or are there generation gaps? If we believe Alvin Toffler, in his <u>Future Shock</u>, we must prepare ourselves for even more generation gaps. The important element in the socialization of humans is, increasingly, time rather than space. This means that the differences between people are going to be the result, not of <u>where</u> you live, but of <u>when</u> you live. Already we are beginning to see that a five-year span between two teenagers can produce startling differences between them. As we pointed out in Chapter 9, hit songs and rock groups now enjoy a very limited life expectancy. Very possibly, the popular longevity of a Bing Crosby or a Frank Sinatra never will be seen again. Young people consume rock groups the way little children consume candy, with <u>change</u> now exalted as a god in our technological society.

To complicate the problem further, age stratification is being institutionalized. For example, how many different age classifications can your students think of? Have them visit the local department stores and list the age classifications used there. A partial list of such categories would include infant, toddler, pre-schooler, kindergartner, pre-teen, sub-teen, post-teen, college set, young adult, young marrieds, etc. "Sun cities" are only for those over a certain age, and some of the "golden years" retirement subdivisions have strict age requirements which limit the length of time young people may visit. We see entire suburbs where people in their 20s, 30s, and early 40s live in tract homes with their children — and it is conceivable that there is not one "old" person living within miles of the subdivision. Two more generational institutions recently have made an appearance — the "swinging singles" apartment complex and the "singles" bars. Obviously, when people are stratified by class, race, or age and are driven to associate with their own group to the exclusion of others, the kind of interaction which leads to personal relationships and to human understanding is not encouraged. This chapter suggests how science fiction may be used to approach the study of generation gaps. Additional complication of the problem, increasing life expectancy, is explored in Kurt Vonnegut's "Tomorrow, and Tomorrow, and Tomorrow." We will see some really serious generational difficulties in this story because the perfection of an elixir allows one to prolong life for hundreds of years.

Student Response:

Ask students what family life would be like if people could live to be 200 years old. What generation problems might result? Would it be proper to end human life at a predetermined point, an age of 200 years, for example, even if an individual were still mentally and physically sound? If people lived to be this old, what might happen to the country's birth rate? Have students write an Sf story based on the idea that no family may have a baby until someone else in the family dies. What kinds of pressure might be exerted upon healthy oldsters to convince them to terminate their lives?

Coping with Increases in Life Expectancy

In the Vonnegut story mentioned above, Grandpa is the oldest member of a muti-generational family, all of whom live in the same cramped apartment. Because of his age, Grandpa has his own private room; this arrangement denies adequate living space to the other family members. One honeymooning couple, for example, is forced to sleep in the hallway in front of the bathroom. Out of frustration, one of the family members waters down Grandpa's elixir, causing a serious altercation and leading eventually to a police raid.

Student Response:

What kinds of strains might a family be subject to when more than two of its generations live together? Why does this happen? How can these strains be alleviated? Ask students to interview a person over 65. What are his values? Worries? Delights? How does he feel about "young" people? As Erik Erikson suggests, there are certain types of people who come to the end of their lives and look back with bitterness and despair: "Life was no damn good to me." Others look back with a certain degree of integrity and wisdom. Have students speculate on why some older people seem to be wise, while others are so bitter.

146

In the Willowbrook Survey, 91 of the respondents indicated that they got along well with older people, excluding parents; only 35 indicated that they were considerably or even somewhat concerned about generation problems. Do we, then, have a situation here in which the media are creating the generation problems? Is it possible that the problem exists only in the minds of older people — or, perhaps, do young people tend to minimize it?

Communicating Between Generations.

The difficulty of communication between generations is likely to increase as our technology grows more complicated, and it certainly is complicated enough already. Sons and daughters are holding jobs which didn't exist just a few short years ago. Not only is it difficult for older people to grasp the life styles of the young, but now it is even difficult for older people to understand what their offspring do for a living, and vice versa. As a result, communication between generations decreases even further. In societies based on the traditional roles of hunting and gathering, children participate very early in the real world of the home and hunt; they learn about this world from close contact with their parents, for parents are the obvious source of such practical information. When America was primarily an agricultural nation, sons worked the fields with their father, and the daughter learned the household chores from her mother. In our present society, however, we see father and son and, increasingly, mother and daughter, going their separate ways in the work world.

A generation-gap problem with an unusual twist is "Absalom," by Henry Kuttner. In this story, a father attempts to prevent his 8-year-old son from learning entropic logic because he is afraid the study will do psychological damage to the boy. The boy, being a genius, is more advanced intellectually than his father was at the same age, so the son strikes out on his own. With the help of another very young genius, he performs a kind of lobotomy upon the father, thereby preventing him from holding back his son. Finally, the father exists only to live vicariously through his son's glory.

Student Response:

Can students think of instances when they thought they were ready for experiences from which their parents were trying to protect them? Clearly, today's young people are experiencing many things at a much younger age than their parents and, certainly, their grandparents did. The so-called sexual revolution dramatically illustrates this point. What do students think the parents' function should be? Should parents try to protect their children from some of life's hard knocks?

The Effect on Adults of a Youth-Oriented Society

In Clancy O'Brien's "Generation Gaps," the society is on such a youth kick that older people are forced into drugs and other youth-related experiences. Because this story is a bit risque in spots, it should be carefully used; however, it does pose some interesting problems for consideration. One of the comments frequently heard from today's teenagers is that they wish their mothers and fathers would act their own age. The parent who insists on dancing the current dance, or listening to the latest song, causes some teens to feel that there has been generational invasion into their own territory. When the Beatles, for example, first became popular, adults turned from them with a certain lack of interest, but once the Beatles became so widely accepted that the Boston Pops was playing their songs, some young people felt that the Beatles no longer were "theirs." One student summed up this attitude toward generational invasion by stating that her mother wore more suede than she herself did — and obviously she resented this "appropriation" of young people's attire.

Student Response:

Should certain experiences be related only to one generation? Should parents try to "understand" their children to the point of actively sharing in their interests, or should parents simply be bystanders in their children's lives?

In Maggie Nadler's "The Pill," a youth drug has been invented which keeps people physically young, although they still can deteriorate mentally to the point of senility. In this story, one 90-year-old who has tapped the fountain of youth still has the body and features of a 20-year-old. Unfortunately, she also has reached the point of drooling senility, so she is committed to a nursing home. Ironically, the woman who commits her has refused to take "the pill" — and thus looks every year of her middle age; as a result, she is scorned by other women, while the 90-year-old is accepted as "normal."

What do you think of such a pill? How might it change our society? In the story, for example, one youthful-looking 50-year-old has a date with a college junior. Ask students to find, in newspaper, magazine, or television advertisements, examples of how youth is "sold" to consumers. Have students make a list of advertised products which specifically appeal to one's desire to remain young. What words and images are used in these ads? Simone de Beauvoir and Susan Sontang have stressed that only beautiful young women are used to model for advertisements. Middle-aged men sometimes are seen selling shirts, cars, cigarettes, or whisky, but middle-aged women rarely are seen in advertisements. Can students explain why?

Dealing with the Problems of the Aged

What to do about the aged? This has become a question of no small importance in our country. As more people enter their 60s, 70s, and 80s, thanks to the wonders of modern medicine, a whole new field of geriatrics has arisen to deal with the problems of the aged. Nursing homes have become a virtual institution in this country to provide care for the oldsters in their remaining years. In "Golden Acres," by Kit Reed, we are offered a depressing solution to the problem of what to do about the older person who no longer can take care of himself. "Golden Acres" is just one more old-age farm; the twist here is that, although residents pay $10,000 for comfort and care for their remaining days, only in the rest home contract's fine print, which is too small for most of them to read, are they told that when they have used up their money for medicine, the death cart will come clattering down the hall to take them away to be incinerated.

Equally depressing is Ron Goulart's "Terminal,"
in which the aged are sent to "Senior Citizens' Terminals"
to have their social utility evaluated. The lives of those
who are found to be socially useless are terminated, very
efficiently, by gas. The interesting twist to this story is
that a 34-year-old man, who is trapped inadvertently within
the system, also is terminated very efficiently.

Student Response:

Is this story so far-fetched? Don't many of us already
judge the old as being useless? Sure, sometimes we permit
them to baby sit, but most older people spend their remaining
years in loneliness and despair. Why, in your students'
opinion, are some old people so vital, while others are not?
What qualities do students most admire in the old? Which
qualities do they admire least? Why are we, as a people,
so afraid of aging?

Why have nursing homes arisen in such numbers in
the United States? Can students think of other, more positive,
ways of caring for the aged? The Hottentots who live in the
region around the Kalahari Desert take their old people, those
who no longer can function, out to the desert and leave them
for the animals and the elements. The Eskimos do much the
same thing; they take their aged out and leave them on ice floes.
On the other hand, the traditional Chinese have had such respect for the elderly that even senility did not preclude respect for them. While Americans might react negatively to
the treatment of the aged by the Hottentots and Eskimos, they
have arrived at humane solutions given the options available
to them. How about us? Are nursing homes more humane than
abandonment on an ice floe?
an ice floe?

Psychological Aspects of Aging

In recent years it has been argued that aging is not just a physical process but a psychological one as well. Some psychologists have become very much interested in what they call "premature" aging. We all know the type of person who, like the man in John Updike's poem, "Ex-Basketball Player," stops growing at adolescence and spends the rest of his life listening to the nostalgic echoes of the basketball crowd and the sweet melodies of the senior prom. Such people see their horizons behind them rather than in the years yet to come.

Student Response:

Robert Kastenbaum, a psychologist, asks people two questions — how long they expect to live, and how long they want to live. Up to 25 percent of his respondents indicate they would like to die before their time. Why might this be? In an article in Psychology Today, "Age: Getting There Ahead Of Time" (December, 1971), Kastenbaum elaborates on his experiments in order to help younger people pre-experience what aging is all about.

Ask your students to select what they expect to be the three most important years of their lives. These years may be in the future or lie in the past. We all know the person who, at age 25, selects all three ages in the past.

Max Weber, the famous sociologist, always maintained that if we really are to understand others, we must put ourselves in their place. Needless to say, this projection is most difficult, but all of us must try. What, for example, about the very young? Can we understand them any better than we can the very old? A pre-schooler described this problem to us very succinctly one day: "Little people have feelings, too," she said. Perhaps with the very young, as with the old, we forget this universal truth too often.

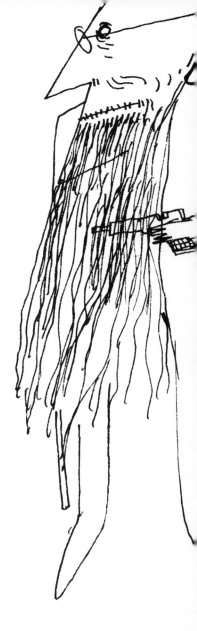

Viewing the World Through a Child's Eyes

In Kris Neville's "From the Government Printing Office," we see the world through the eyes of a three-year-old child who has some bitterly telling and funny comments to make about his parents. Ask students to try to write an Sf short story in which they view an experience through the eyes of a one-month-old baby, a three-year-old, a 10-year-old. One student project which was most revealing was a short film in which two students pretended they were children riding in a car's baby seat. As the car moved down the street, all that could be seen was the sky, the roofs of buildings, and treetops. Think of how a child must feel, always having to look up at table tops, people, etc. Have students try to find other ways of experiencing the viewpoint of a child.

Perhaps the best Sf now being written about children is by Zenna Henderson, the author of the novel The People. Her short stories exhibit a rare sensitivity towards children. In her collection Holding Wonder, she offers a varied and stimulating sampling of her work. In "Loo Ree," for example, a child's imaginary playmate turns out to be an extraterrestrial being who approaches the child's teacher one day and asks to be taught how to read. Goosebumps creep up your arms when you read this story, but it has a fine message.

Perhaps the teacher also might want to use Ray Bradbury's "All Summer in a Day" (cited in Chapter 8) with this chapter, for it, too, offers a sensitive insight into the world of the child. Bradbury also has written "Hail and Farewell," a story about a 40-year-old man who looks like a boy of 12. The man/boy dedicates his life to bringing joy to childless couples; he travels from town to town, staying with such couples for a few years until they discover his secret, and then he moves on.

One other suggestion, although it is not really Sf, is Ray Bradbury's Dandelion Wine, a delightful and nostalgic journey into an Illinois childhood of the past. The reader is allowed to sniff freshly-mown grass, unmasked by gasoline fumes, and to experience a child's own private "time machine," a very old man who has excellent recall and who fascinates the child with stories of his long life. It's too bad our society doesn't pay more attention to other living "time machines."

Traveling Through Time

One final way of approaching the theme of the relationships between generations is developed in some time-travel stories. In Bradbury's "Time in Thy Flight," for example, two youngsters from the future are brought back, as a school assignment, to the year 1928. The students and their adult chaperone are to observe the way the people of that year live; in effect, this is the children's final exam. At first, they are appalled as they watch a circus, see caged animals for the first time, and are repulsed by the animal odors. But the more they observe, the more enchanted by 1928 they become, to the point that they resist going home to the future — much to the chagrin of their chaperone.

Student Response:

If you could live in any age, when would you want to live? Why? Have students pick one time in the past and one in the future. What would life be like at these times? What differences would you expect to find from your former life style? What new attitudes? What new opinions? Using the time-travel idea, have each student select some older person to interview. Ask students to recapture how this person felt when he was their age. Remind students to listen carefully because they are being asked to put themselves in the place of the person they're interviewing. In a separate assignment, tell students to project themselves into the future in which their children and grandchildren will be living — to pretend this is the year 2000 or 2050. What do the students' offspring look like? How do they dress? What are their everyday lives like? What are their values?

Avoiding a Future War Between Generations

What might the generation gaps of the future be like? Let us hope that Clifford Simak's "Day of Truce" proves wrong. In this story, outright war has erupted between the younger generations, known as "the punks," and the older generations who own the few remaining suburban estates. Most of the estates have been stormed, burned, and dismantled by the young vandals; those which remain standing are heavily barricaded behind electric fences. The story is concerned with the "day of truce," the one day each year when the war is halted and the older generations follow the ritual of inviting "the punks" into their homes for a day of feasting and dancing. The conclusion of the story sees the "day of truce" over, and "the punks" readying themselves for still one more assault on the estate.

Student Response:

Do students think it is conceivable that generational differences could lead to violence? How about verbal violence? Can students think of any incidents in which they have heard or seen generational violence? How might the present ways in which generations get along together be improved? What contributions could older people make to students' lives? What contributions could students make to older people? Should man attempt to balance communities so that age stratification doesn't result? What other kinds of solutions for generation gaps can students think of?

Bibliography

Bradbury, Ray, "All Summer in a Day," Tomorrow's
 Children, Isaac Asimov (ed.), Doubleday.
———, Dandelion Wine, Bantam.
———, "Hail and Farewell," S Is for Space, Doubleday.
———, "Time in Thy Flight," S Is for Space, Doubleday.
Goulart, Ron, "Terminal," Broke Down Engine and Other
 Troubles with Machines, Colliers.
Henderson, Zenna, Holding Wonder, Avon.
Kuttner, Henry, "Absalom," Social Education (February,
1973); also in Tomorrow the Stars, Robert Heinlein (ed.),
Berkley. Nadler, Maggie, "The Pill," Fantastic: Science
Fiction and Fantasy Stories, (April, 1972).
Neville, Kris, "From the Government Printing Office,"
 Dangerous Visions, Harlan Ellison (ed.), Berkley.
O'Brien, Clancy, "Generation Gaps," Analog, (September,
 1972).
Reed, Kit, "Golden Acres," Voyages: Scenarios for a Ship
 Called Earth, Rob Sauer (ed.), Ballantine; also in Above
 the Human Landscape, Willis McNelly and Leon Stover
 (eds.), Goodyear.
Simak, Clifford, "Day of Truce," Nightmare Age, Frederik
 Pohl (ed.), Ballantine.
Vonnegut, Kurt, "Tomorrow, Tomorrow, Tomorrow,"
 Eco-Fiction, John Stadler (ed.), Washington Square Press;
 also in Welcome to the Monkey House, Dell.

APPENDIX 1: WHAT IF . . . ? EXERCISES

As we have indicated throughout the book, "What If...?" exercises may be used in a variety of ways to stimulate students to think about the future. In Chapter 1, for example, we suggested that these exercises be used to spark creativity. They also may be used to complement stories such as "Gadget vs. Trend" (see Chapter 4) to help students select a problem and, through extrapolation, project the consequences to their absurd point. In this way, students are encouraged to become more divergent and less convergent in their thinking; thus, their options for the future are increased.

If discussion is slow on any of the exercises, present a series of key questions. For example: What would be the consequences of installing mini-computers in each home for the purpose of democratically sampling the will of the people on national issues? Would Congress' function change? If so, how? Might the nation's political parties change? Do we really want the "people" to vote on all issues? Which issues wouldn't you want the people to vote on? Can you think of any ways to "get around" the computers? Might there be conspiracies to rig the machines? Would television have to change its format and become more educational and less entertaining? In other words, would T.V. have a greater responsibility to keep people aware of the day's issues?

What If . . . ?

1. A pollution-free electric car were perfected which could reach speeds comparable to those of present cars and could be re-charged every 300 miles for the same price as a tank of gasoline?
2. Every family was limited to only one car?
3. Drivers' tests were eliminated and a special device was installed in each car to tally up each driver's mistakes? After a certain point, the car would shut off for that particular driver.
4. A machine were invented which could predict with absolute accuracy the date of a person's death? Would you want to know when you would die?
5. Before people could marry, they had to submit to a computer-administered test on 100 correlates of compatibility?

(Ask students to decide what a passing score would be. What items should appear on the test?)

6. The atomic bomb and other nuclear weapons were eliminated?

7. Every citizen could install in his home a mini-computer to use in voting on key national issues such as: "Shall we go to war with Power A?"

8. All sports became T.V. sports, with no live audiences? With android teams?

9. Robots took over most of the menial tasks now performed by humans?

10. People were able to be made invisible?

11. A television set could be programmed to watch you, no matter where you were in your house?

12. People could travel through time and space? Where and when would you want to go? Why?

13. Brain transplants were perfected?

14. An individual were allowed to terminate his life at will? Might suicide parlors be established for this purpose?

15. Geneticists discovered how to create human life in a test tube?

16. You could receive an injection which would make it impossible for you to conceive or father a child for one year?

17. Your body could be frozen, and you could be awakened hundreds of years from now? Would you elect to be frozen if you were in good health? When would you want to be awakened?

18. Communications were established with porpoises, which were found to have very high intelligence?

19. Communications were established with other worlds? Should we trust them? Should they trust us?

20. Men learned how to bypass human speech, and could communicate on higher planes comparable to ESP?

21. People lived to be hundreds of years old? Would you want to live this long if you were guaranteed that you always could look youthful?

22. Drugs were dispensed in local speed-a-bars, similar to present-day cocktail lounges?

23. People were forced to live in 1,000-story buildings in the urban regions of the country?

24. People were paid for their labor on a social utility scale? (The person who contributes the most to society, regardless of how mundane his tasks, would be paid the most. Garbage men could earn as much as doctors.)

157

25. At 18, each person would appear at a central terminal to be programmed for the work he or she would do for the rest of his life?

26. Conventional prisons were eliminated in favor of other forms of controlling criminals? (One suggestion might be to place electrodes in the criminal's brain; if he strays from the territory assigned to him, terrible pains would shoot through his body and drive him back to "home territory."

27. Electrodes, placed within a person's body, could serve as his particular form of identification, thus eliminating the use of credit cards? (This idea is being worked on at present.)

28. Cloning were possible? Would you want to be duplicated? What might some of the consequences of this process be? Should men like Albert Einstein be duplicated? Is there anyone you would not want to be duplicated? Why?

29. We were able to predict, with absolute accuracy, which human embryoes were healthy and which were not? Should we then eliminate the unhealthy ones? Should this be a question answered only by the parents? By the doctors? Should society, as a whole, have a voice in the decision?

30. The great majority of people stopped reading and received their entertainment, news, and other knowledge through media such as television and films?

What If...?

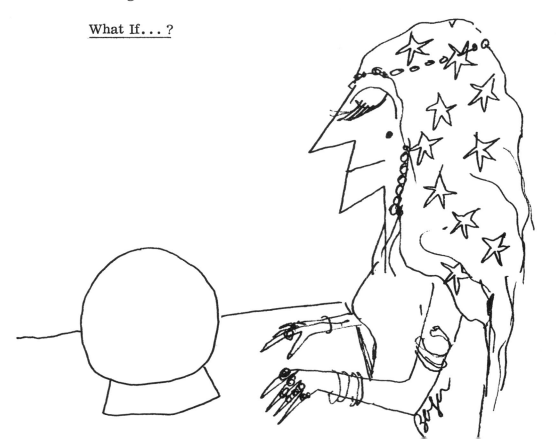

APPENDIX 2: WILLOWBROOK SURVEY

As the Introduction says, we gave the following survey to collect both demographic and attitudinal data. We have a senior class of approximately 700 students. We decided to sample approximately one-third of them, selecting every third name from the grade book of each teacher who taught Senior Social Science, a required course for all seniors. (Although we could have used a table of random numbers, we felt that at this time this was not necessary.) Since the survey form is relatively brief, it takes only about ten minutes to complete.

As in most attitudinal surveys, correlating data are important. For the SES (socioeconomic status) question, Question No. 2 (How would you best describe your father's job?), for example, some suggestions follow. Do more blue or white collar families own two or more cars? Which occupational groups have the larger families? Which groups are most concerned about population control? Which groups would use public transportation more?

The number of students answering appears right after the category in each question; the number in parentheses is the percentage of students responding to that part of the question. A student's omission of an answer is indicated by a zero, followed by the number not answering. "N," of course, stands for the total number of students taking the survey.

Where to go from here? One possibility is to give a post-test to selected students after they experience the units in this book. We would expect that, as a result of the units, students might check more problems that they are concerned about and even show more pessimism towards solving these problems. But as suggested in the Introduction, pessimism can be an effective catalyst for change.

THE WILLOWBROOK SURVEY

Answer the following questions by choosing the one response
which best represents your thinking.

1. Sex
    1. male 94 (49%)   2. female 98 (51%)

2. How would you best describe your father's job?
    1. managerial (store manager, etc.) 24 (13%)
    2. professional (doctor, lawyer, etc.) 18 (9%)
    3. sales (salesman, real estate agent, etc.) 23 (12%)
    4. self-employed (owns his own business) 15 (8%)
    5. technical (engineer, computer technician, etc.) 42 (22%)
    6. trades (carpenter, plumber, etc.) 21 (11%)
    7. others (all other kinds of job) 36 (19%)
    8. does not apply 10 (5%)

$$9 = 1 \qquad 0 = 2$$

3. How many brothers and sisters do you have?
    0. none 6 (3%) 1. one 33 (17%) 2. two 43 (22%)
    3. three 43 (22%) 4. four or more 67 (36%)

4. How many cars does your family own?
    0. none 0 (0%) 1. one 29 (15%) 2. two 100 (52%)
    3. three 34 (18%) 4. four or more 29 (15%)

5. How many hours a week do you spend on cars? (driving,
   fixing, etc.)
    0. none 20 (10%) 1. five hours or less 68 (36%)
    2. six to ten hours 41 (21%) 3. eleven to fifteen
    hours 25 (13%) 4. more than fifteen hours 38 (20%)

6. Which of the following statements best expresses your
   attitude toward America's future?
    1. I am generally optimistic that the country can solve
       its social problems. 108 (57%)
    2. I am generally pessimistic that the country can solve
       its social problems. 45 (23%)
    3. No opinion. 38 (20%)

Indicate your degree of concern about the following problems:

7. Too many automobiles
    1. not at all concerned 35 (18%) 2. somewhat concerned 94 (49%) 3. considerably concerned 42 (22%)
    4. very concerned   20   (11%)

    $$0 = 1$$

8. Environmental pollution (water, air, landscape)
    1. not at all concerned 5 (3%) 2. somewhat concerned 33 (17%) 3. considerably concerned 70 (36%) 4. very concerned 84 (44%)

9. Population problems (specifically, that the suburbs and cities are becoming crowded)
    1. not at all concerned 18 (9%) 2. somewhat concerned 77 (40%) 3. considerably concerned 57 (30%)
    4. very concerned 40 (21%)

10. The possibility of atomic war
    1. not at all concerned 43 (23%) 2. somewhat concerned 70 (37%) 3. considerably concerned 28 (14%)
    4. very concerned 50 (26%)

    $$0 = 1$$

11. Generation problems (people of different ages don't seem to understand one another)
    1. not at all concerned 46 (24%) 2. somewhat concerned 70 (41%) 3. considerably concerned 44 (23%)
    4. very concerned 23 (12%)

12. The increasing number and use of machines and computers (people don't seem to be able to cope with this highly mechanized world)
    1. not at all concerned 72 (38%) 2. somewhat concerned 72 (38%) 3. considerably concerned 31 (16%)
    4. very concerned 17 (8%)

13. Increasing numbers of people who disobey regulations and laws
    1. not at all concerned 24 (13%) 2. somewhat concerned 66 (34%) 3. considerably concerned 59 (30%)
    4. very concerned 45 (23%)

14. Worsening relations between suburbs and cities (cities and suburbs are growing farther apart)
1. not at all concerned 105 (55%) 2. somewhat concerned 64 (33%) 3. considerably concerned 15 (8%)
4. very concerned 8 (4%)

15. Differences in income among social levels (the rich get richer and the poor get poorer)
1. not at all concerned 23 (12%) 2. somewhat concerned 74 (39%) 3. considerably concerned 56 (29%)
4. very concerned 39 (20%)

16. At the present, how much do you feel that you, as an individual, can do to solve the problems mentioned above?
1. no influence at all 72 (38%) 2. some influence 111 (58%) 3. quite a bit of influence 9 (4%)

17. In the future, when you've finished your education, how much do you feel that you, as an individual, might do to solve the problems mentioned above?
1. no influence at all 31 (16%) 2. some influence 133 (70%) 3. quite a bit of influence 27 (14%)
                    0 = 1

18. If public transportation were made as cheap and available as the automobile, to what extent would you use it?
1. I would rarely, if ever, use it   50   (26%)
2. I would use it somewhat   67   (35%)
3. I would use it considerably   42   (22%)
4. I would use it as much as I possibly could   33   (17%)

19. The number of automobiles in this country should be limited to one per family.
1. yes 17 (9%) 2. no 141 (73%) 3. no opinion 34 (18%)

20. Some kind of strict pressure, either from the government or from some other agency, should be used to help keep the suburbs and cities from becoming overcrowded.
1. yes 68 (36%) 2. no 69 (36%) 3. no opinion 54 (28%)
                    0 = 1

21. Stiff fines and/or jail sentences should be imposed
    against polluters, whether corporations or individuals.
    1. yes 147 (76%) 2. no 5 (3%) 3. not sure 37 (19%)
    4. no opinion 3 (2%)

22. I would be in favor of returnable containers only for food
    and drinks.
    1. yes 106 (55%) 2. no 30 (16%) 3. not sure 46
    (24%) 4. no opinion 10 (5%)

23. This country should be willing to share its wealth more
    equally among the different levels of society.
    1. yes 94 (49%) 2. no 28 (15%) 3. not sure 52 (27%)
    4. no opinion 18 (9%)

24. The United States should be willing to give up its atomic
    weapons even if no other country does.
    1. yes 10 (5%) 2. no 122 (64%) 3. not sure 51 (27%)
    4. no opinion 8 (4%)
                    0 = 1

25. We, as a people, should be more concerned about law
    and order.
    1. yes 145 (76%) 2. no 14 (7%) 3. not sure 20 (11%)
    4. no opinion 12 (6%)
                    0 = 1

26. I generally get along well with people older than myself
    (not counting parents).
    1. yes 175 (91%) 2. no 3 (2%) 3. not sure 11 (6%)
    4. no opinion 2 (1%)
                    0 = 1

27. I think that America should limit its use of machines
    and computers.
    1. yes 44 (23%) 2. no 87 (46%) 3. not sure 46 (24%)
    4. no opinion 14 (7%)
                    0 = 1

N = 192

APPENDIX 3: SIMULATION EXERCISE

The following simulation exercise was designed and used by us in a "Caste and Class" unit. As suggested in Chapter 8, we recommend it be used after the class has discussed Huxley's book.

Rules of the exercise:

1. The time required: one day. To be taken as an in-school field trip.
2. On the previous day, students will draw slips of paper which will assign them to their caste: Alpha, Beta, Gamma, Delta, or Epsilon. They will be told at this time how to dress for the next day and will be given a list of services for which they will have to pay and a notation of how much each of these services will cost. (Some examples: lunch, pass privileges, washroom privileges, et. al.)
3. Teachers and administrators will be contacted the week before the exercise and asked if they will (1) accept student help in various capacities and (2) assume the responsibility of paying the student in chits — a certain amount of an agreed-upon medium of exchange. *
4. Jobs for low caste students will be less desirable to perform and will be rewarded correspondingly less in chits than the higher caste jobs.
5. At the end of the day, a system of rewards will be applied to the students according to the number of chits they have been able to accumulate during the day.
6. A set of readings will be given to the Alphas and Betas during the day, and they will be asked to study them. A quiz on the readings will be given to all students the next day. The readings, of course, represent forms of education to which the lower castes have little access. The lower caste groups should do considerable complaining.
7. Late in the day, several interviews will be scheduled with Epsilons. Their responses will be taped for later use in the unit. This debriefing generally indicates the students' displeasure with the handicaps imposed upon them. Hopefully, some insights into how it feels to be subjected to discrimination will result. To precipitate

discussion, we also play the tapes to those not of Epsilon status and in this way all students vicariously experience the Epsilons' frustrations.

*It would be best if all available jobs are advertised via a mimeographed sheet posted at various times and places during the course of the day. Of course, certain duties are to be performed only by Alphas, Betas, etc., and should be advertised as such. A good idea of which group should perform which jobs can be arrived at by jotting down student opinions, during the early days of the unit, as they talk about the kinds of jobs each group might hold. The students, of course, shouldn't be let in on the fact that they eventually will be called upon to perform these various duties.

APPENDIX 4: QUESTIONS

We use the following general questions with novels and major feature-length films. Keep in mind that not all questions can be used with every novel and film. These questions are used primarily to spark discussion.

Economic: What is considered wealth in this society? (The one depicted in book or film?) Who produces and who consumes the products?

Political: How is order kept in the society? Who has the power? What allowance is made for the deviant or non-conformist? What sort of leader is considered "good"? What role does the military play? What would pose the greatest threat to the society? Why? What is the author's conception of man: Is man basically good? Bad? Trustful?

Social: What classes exist? How does one gain and lose status? Is status ascribed or achieved? In other words, does one gain status by birth or can one work his way up? How difficult is it to move from one class to another? What is the place of the family?

Religious: What religious beliefs prevail? What is the role of a supernatural being? How is the religion organized? Who holds the most religious power in the society?

Artistic: Is any allowance made for artistic and aesthetic expression? What kinds of art, music, literature, if any, exist in the society? What role does the government play in controlling artistic and aesthetic expression?

Other Cultures: How does the society view other societies? Suspiciously?

General: How would you like living in this particular society? What would you find most distasteful about it? What would you find most enjoyable about it? If you could change one thing in the society, what would you change and why? What would pose the greatest threat to the society? Why? To what extent do you see present-day American society in the story? What would have to specifically happen for American society to become like the story? How might this be prevented?

Also for novels and feature films, we employ a like scale. Students are asked to rank all the major characters in the work from the one they like the best to the one they like the least. Of course, during discussion students must justify their ratings.

167

The Authors

Bernard Hollister's degrees are a B.A. (History), Roosevelt University, Chicago; M.A. (History), Northern Illinois University; and M.S.T. (Sociology), Illinois Institute of Technology. He has participated in NDEA Summer Institutes in American History, University of Chicago, and Middle Eastern Affairs, Rutgers University; and NDEA Academic Year Institute (part-time) in world history, University of Chicago; and a National Science Foundation Academic Year in Sociology at Illinois Institute of Technology. He was a John Hay Summer Fellow (Charles Keller Award); has taught science fiction at Willowbrook High School, Villa Park, Illinois, and a course for teachers at National College of Education, Chicago. His articles include "Violence: A Selective Bibliography", Media and Methods; "Grokking the Future", Media and Methods; "Who Am I?", Media and Methods (forthcoming); and "What If?". Futures Conditional.

Deane C. Thompson has an M.A. in Education from the University of Wisconsin, and another in history from Loyola University. He has taught at Chicago Latin School as well as at Willowbrook. In the summer of 1969, Mr. Thompson was a participant in the summer writing program of the Amherst project, and in 1970 he received a Coe Fellowship in American History. In summer of 1971 he had an institute in Asian Studies at the University of Hawaii.

168

Date Due

JAN 22 '78		
OCT 26 1978		
NOV 2 1980		
LIMITED		
RESERVE		
APR 1 9 1981		
MY 2 9 '81		
MAY 3 1 '86		
APR 02 '91		
MAY 31 '92		
MAR 2 7 1998		

PRINTED IN U.S.A.   CAT. NO. 24 161   BRO DART